WITHDRAWN

282.73
Wei   Weigel, George

             Freedom and its
             discontents

DUE DATE

FREEDOM
AND ITS
DISCONTENTS

OTHER BOOKS BY GEORGE WEIGEL

*Peace and Freedom: Christian Faith, Democracy,
and the Problem of War*

*Tranquillitas Ordinis: The Present Failure and
Future Promise of American Catholic Thought
on War and Peace*

Catholicism and the Renewal of American Democracy

*American Interests, American Purpose:
Moral Reasoning and U.S. Foreign Policy*

*Fieles y Libres: Catolicismo, Derechos Humanos,
y Democracia*

*Retos Contemporáneos: Reflexiones desde
el realismo bíblico de la tradición católico*
(Editor)

*A Century of Catholic Social Thought: Essays on
'Rerum Novarum' and Nine Other Key Documents*
(Editor, with Robert Royal)

*The American Search for Peace: Moral Reasoning,
Religious Hope, and National Security*
(Editor, with John Langan, S.J.)

GEORGE WEIGEL is president of the Ethics and Public Policy
Center. A graduate of St. Mary's Seminary and University in
Baltimore and the University of St. Michael's College in
Toronto, he was a 1984–85 Fellow of the Woodrow Wilson
International Center for Scholars.

FREEDOM AND ITS DISCONTENTS

Catholicism Confronts Modernity

GEORGE WEIGEL

ETHICS AND PUBLIC POLICY CENTER

The **ETHICS AND PUBLIC POLICY CENTER,** established in 1976, conducts a program of research, writing, publications, and conferences to encourage debate on domestic and foreign policy issues among religious, educational, academic, business, political, and other leaders. A nonpartisan effort, the Center is supported by contributions (which are tax deductible) from foundations, corporations, and individuals. The authors alone are responsible for the views expressed in Center publications.

Library of Congress Cataloging-in-Publication Data

Weigel, George.
Freedom and its discontents : Catholicism confronts modernity / George Weigel.
p.   cm.
Includes bibliographical references and index.
   1. Catholic Church—United States—History—1965-
2. Liberty—Religious aspects—Catholic Church.
3. Liberty—Religious aspects—Christianity.
4. Catholic Church—Doctrines.   I. Title.
BX1406.2.W46   1991   282' .73'09045—dc20   91-13458 CIP

ISBN 0–89633–158–X (cloth)
ISBN 0–89633–159–8 (paper)

Distributed by arrangement with:
National Book Network
4720 Boston Way
Lanham, MD 20706

All Ethics and Public Policy Center books are produced on acid-free paper. The paper used in this publication meets the minimum requirements of American National Standard for Information Sciences—Permanence of Paper for Printed Library Materials, ANSI Z39.48–1984.   ∞™

Ethics and Public Policy Center
1030 Fifteenth Street N.W.
Washington, D.C. 20005
(202) 682–1200

Freedom is not the power of doing what we like, but the right of being able to do what we ought.

—LORD ACTON

Among the many admirable values of this nation there is one that stands out in particular. It is freedom. The concept of freedom is part of the very fabric of this nation as a political community of free people. Freedom is a great gift, a blessing of God.

From the beginning of America, freedom was directed to forming a well-ordered society and to promoting its peaceful life. Freedom was channeled to the fullness of human life, to the preservation of human dignity, and to the safeguarding of all human rights. An experience of ordered freedom is truly a part of the cherished history of this land.

This is the freedom that America is called to live and guard and to transmit. She is called to exercise it in such a way that it will also benefit the cause of freedom in other nations and among other peoples. The only true freedom, the only freedom that can truly satisfy, is the freedom to do what we ought as human beings created by God according to his plan. It is the freedom to live out the truth of what we are and who we are before God, the truth of our identity as children of God, as brothers and sisters in a common humanity.

—POPE JOHN PAUL II

O beautiful for pilgrims' feet
Whose stern, impassioned stress
A thoroughfare for freedom beat
Across the wilderness;
America, America,
God mend thine every flaw,
Confirm thy soul in self-control,
Thy liberty in law.

—KATHARINE LEE BATES

Magistris nostris reverentia

For

+ Sister Mary Moira, S.S.N.D.
  Sister Miriam Jude, S.S.N.D.
  Evelyn A. Donohoe
  Sister George Mary, S.S.N.D.
  Sister Mary Enda, S.S.N.D.
  Victor B. Galeone

Lawrence T. Kowalski
W. Vincent Bechtel
William M. Thompson
Francis I. Kane
James B. Dunning
Daniel L. Donovan

Contents

Acknowledgments

Many friends and colleagues have shared in the preparation of these essays. Peter Berger, Avery Dulles, S.J., John Farina, James Finn, Philip Gleason, Mary Ann Glendon, J. Bryan Hehir, David Hollenbach, Henry Hyde, Francis Kane, Joseph A. Komonchak, John Langan, S.J., William J. Lee, S.S., James W. Lothamer, S.S., Richard John Neuhaus, David Novak, Michael Novak, James Nuechterlein, Marvin O'Connell, Robert Pickus, Brad Roberts, Robert Royal, J. Francis Stafford, and William Thompson have been important partners in the conversations that helped shape the arguments here.

Special gratitude is owed to the following:

Richard John Neuhaus, who invited me to prepare a paper on religious liberty for a 1987 conference on "the structure of freedom" sponsored by the (late) Center on Religion and Society and the Institute for the Study of Economic Culture.

Thomas Gannon, S.J., Gordon Anderson, and the Professors World Peace Academy, who invited me to prepare a paper on Catholicism and democracy for a 1989 conference in London.

Peter Berger, who invited me to prepare a paper on American Catholicism and an ethic of wealth creation for a 1989 conference sponsored by the Institute for the Study of Economic Culture and the Institute of Contemporary Thought.

R. Bruce Douglass, John Langan, S.J., and the Committee on Catholic Studies at Georgetown University, who invited me to prepare a paper on contemporary Catholic intellectual life for a 1989 faculty conference at Georgetown.

Carol Griffith of the Ethics and Public Policy Center was a wise and challenging editor. Christopher Ditzenberger, also of the Center, labored heroically to prepare the manuscript for publication.

I should also like to thank the following for permission to reprint material: the William B. Eerdmans Publishing Company, for "Religious Freedom: The First Human Right"; the Professors World Peace Academy, for "Catholicism and Democracy: The Other Twentieth-Century Revolution"; and the Institute for Contemporary Studies, for "Camels and Needles, Talents and Treasure." I should also note that an earlier version of "The Ecumenism of Time" appeared in the October 1989 issue of *Crisis*, and that parts of "Capturing the Story Line" appeared in the November 1990 issue of *First Things*. Previously published essays have been reworked, in some cases extensively, for this volume.

The venerable principle *magistris nostris reverentia*, "reverence to our masters," prompts me to dedicate this book to twelve teachers whose influence on my life and thought has been longlasting.

GEORGE WEIGEL

Washington, D.C.
Easter, 1991

Introduction

M uch as Father John Courtney Murray predicted in 1966, just a year after the conclusion of the Second Vatican Council, the nature, scope, theological meaning, and political structure of human freedom have become the subjects of continuing debate within the Catholic Church in the United States. The essays in this book attempt to advance that discussion, which has profound implications both for the internal life of the Church and for the Church's address to the world in which it is a pilgrim.

Appropriately enough, in this most persecution-ridden of centuries, the Council's primary text on the freedom of the human person defined the fundamental human right of religious liberty. According to Murray, the Council's *Declaration on Religious Freedom* taught that "in political society the human person is to live his relation with God, or even with his private idol, in freedom—within a zone of freedom juridically guaranteed against invasion by any form of coercion."* This teaching on the private meaning of religious freedom was biblically rooted, although, as Murray freely conceded, it was also the product of "centuries of secular and religious experience" that had been necessary in order to bring the biblical seed to "explicit conceptualization" and a measure of fruition. Thus one dimension of the new Catholic debate over freedom was a fresh and potentially enriched understanding of Christian personalism—traditionally regarded as one of the key building-blocks of Catholic social thought.

---

*John Courtney Murray, S.J., "Freedom, Authority, Community," *America* 115:23 (December 23, 1966), p. 734.

1

The Council also addressed the *public* meaning of the freedom that individual persons enjoyed by reason of their being created in the image and likeness of God. For, as Murray put it, the Council's *Pastoral Constitution on the Church in the Modern World* taught that "the relation of the Church to the world and of the world to the Church is to be lived in freedom." The Church asked of the world nothing but the freedom to live its life as the Body of Christ: in its preaching of the Gospel, in its liturgical and spiritual life, in its "peaceful entry into the political world, there to make moral judgments when political affairs raise moral issues." In turn, the Church acknowledged that "the world" had its own legitimate autonomy, or, in Murray's words, "the world too has its rightful freedom to live its own life—or rather, its many lives: political, economic, social, cultural, scientific—in accordance with [its own] dynamisms and structures." Viewed through this prism, Vatican II posed a basic challenge to the many monisms, religious and secular, ancient and modern, that continued to beset human life and the cause of human freedom. The freedom of the Church and the freedom of the world were both genuine freedoms, for the world was of God just as the Church was of God, although in a different way.

As the essays in Part One argue, this particular word of the Council went forth with a tremendous effect in the lives of men and nations. The Catholic human rights revolution, one of whose foundational documents was surely the *Declaration on Religious Freedom*, has been a crucial (if largely unappreciated) factor in the democratic transitions that are such an important dynamic of world politics. Indeed, the transformation of the Roman Catholic Church from a perceived bastion of the status quo and the *ancien régime* into perhaps the world's foremost institutional proponent of basic human rights has been one of the truly seminal changes in a century whose public life has been characterized far more by change than by continuity.

But there was yet another dimension to the new Catholic encounter with the problem and promise of human freedom: an internal dimension, if you will. As Murray put it, the Council "inevitably raised the . . . question [of] freedom in the Church. Is not the Christian life within the Christian community to be lived in freedom? Even the essential Christian experience of obedience to the authority of the Church—is it not somehow to be an experience of Christian freedom in the evangelical sense?"

While the answer to that general question is surely "yes," it would be very rash indeed to suggest that the ongoing American Catholic reflection on freedom and authority in the Church has been as lucid, moderate, and theologically enriching as Father Murray might have hoped in 1966. There is no need here to revisit the sundry contestations—over contraception, abortion, academic freedom, the Church's ministry, the teaching authority of bishops' conferences—that have, at least according to the press, made dissent from authority, and in fact the radical juxtaposition of "freedom" and "authority," the chief story line of post-Conciliar American Catholicism. It is surely worth noting that, amidst all this controversy, the Church in the United States has remained remarkably vigorous in its parish life, in a living refutation of the claim that modernity, and especially American modernity, necessarily leads to radical forms of secularization. Still, few reasonable observers would claim that the American Catholic Church has gotten its act together, so to speak, on the question of freedom and authority within the Body of Christ.

Happily, there are signs that various extreme positions in that ongoing debate are being marginalized: sometimes by sheer exhaustion, sometimes because of the effective weight of superior argument. Deconstructionists may yet be found in more than a few theology departments on Catholic campuses; but more positive theological reflection, whose aim is to enlarge the Church's acquaintance with the full resources of its rich tradition, is also under way. Some American Catholic historians are busily rewriting the American Catholic story the better to fit the concerns of what the British call the "chattering classes"; but other historians are helping the Church in the United States rediscover, and reappropriate, those crucial elements of its own unique history that bear on the contemporary debate over evangelical freedom. The essays in Part Three of this book try to give those positive impulses in American Catholic intellectual life a bit of a boost.

The debate over the meaning and exercise of human freedom has, of course, a perennial character in these United States. Its participants have included Hamilton and Jefferson, Madison and Mason, Webster and Calhoun, Lincoln and Douglas, Wilson and Lodge, Truman and Taft, Humphrey and Thurmond. Given what seems to be the incorrigibly religious character of the American people, these debates were often informed by biblical religion, and by the moral claims that its various American adherents took to be laid upon them by their Christian and Jewish faiths. And, again contrary to media stereotypes, that is as true today as it was in the Illinois senate campaign of 1858. Post-Conciliar Catholicism has entered that ongoing argument vigorously; the essays in Part Two are a reflection on the Catholic contribution to two crucial component parts of the American struggle with the problem of freedom—America's responsibilities in the world, and the churnings of the American economy.

The future of the quest for a freedom that satisfies the deepest yearnings of the human heart will not be shaped in the United States alone. But it will be profoundly affected by the American debate over how a free people ought to live, as individuals and in community. The United States is, in Ben Wattenberg's happy phrase, the first "universal nation"—a microcosm of the world's struggles with pluralism and community, and a laboratory for testing the ways in which personal freedom can serve the common good. American culture's palpable influence on other cultures throughout the world means that it makes a great deal of difference—for better or for worse, and usually for both—how Americans order their lives and their loves, their loyalties and their responsibilities, in what the Catholic bishops of the United States called, in 1884, "this home of freedom."

And given the "unsecularization" of America, the demographic weight of Catholicism in our society, and the self-consciously public character of modern Catholic social teaching, the American struggle with freedom—with its satisfactions and its discontents—will be significantly shaped by the quality of Catholic reflection on how it is that human beings are truly free.

PART ONE

The Catholic Human Rights Revolution

1

Religious Freedom: The First Human Right

Human rights talk, in both international and domestic public life today, is the occasion for a great deal of special pleading in the name of the "priority" of this, that, or the other putative "right." The problem is not limited to the woollier pronouncements of the United Nations and its agencies. Things have gone so far here at home that, in the debate over Judge Robert Bork's nomination to the Supreme Court and in local elections since the Court's 1989 *Webster* decision, the "right to abortion" has not infrequently been proclaimed by some as the most fundamental personal guarantee under the Constitution of 1787.

There is something quite wrong, conceptually and practically, with the use of rights language as a rhetorical intensifier in partisan political debate. Yet most reasonable people also understand that there is a hierarchy of values among human rights. We know intuitively, for example, that habeas corpus is a more crucial guarantor of individual liberty than the putative "right" to a secondary education. But despite broad agreement on the fact of a hierarchy of rights, there remains a job of sorting out and prioritizing to be done, in the new democracies and even in societies long committed to human freedom. Moreover, the issues engaged here involve more than conceptual propriety; they bear on the very structure of freedom. Do some human rights, if actualized in public life, make possible the honoring of other human rights? To put it more sharply, is there one human right that is the irreducible foundation, the *sine qua non*, of any meaningful scheme of "human rights"?

With due respect for the dangers of special pleading in this complex and volatile field, I will argue that there is. I believe that the right to religious freedom, or, more broadly put, freedom of conscience, is the one absolutely fundamental human right. Let me put the argument into a series of propositions, and then fill out the discussion with two more discursive sections on the priority of religious freedom.

THE INTERIOR MEANING OF RELIGIOUS FREEDOM

1. Human beings are more than individuals; human beings are persons distinguished by an innate capacity for thinking, choosing, and acting, and by an innate drive for meaning and value.

Whether from an anthropological, sociological, philosophical, or theological point of view, the distinguishing characteristics of human beings, as contrasted with other forms of sensate life, are (1) our unquenchable desire to know who we are and what our place is in the order of things (our intellect) and (2) our unquenchable zeal to organize our world according to those understandings (our will). Intellect and will are not epiphenomenal, the expression of other mundane forces (such as economics). Intellect and will are the fundamental, defining characteristics of human personhood. This recognition does not require, though it is supported by, adherence to what believers understand as religious revelation.

2. Freedom to pursue the quest for meaning and value, without coercion, is the fundamental prerequisite to a truly human life.

"Human dignity" often connotes possession of the material necessities of life: food, clothing, and shelter. Yet we know from our own experience, as well as from human history, that the satisfaction of these material needs does not exhaust the meaning of "human dignity." The biblical claim that "man does not live by bread alone" is affirmed far beyond the limits of the Jewish and Christian religious communities. In some modern societies that have done reasonably well in providing material goods—people are not starving or living in the streets, they receive adequate medical care, children do not run around naked—"human dignity" is sorely lacking, a fact evidenced by the people's persistent attempts to leave those societies. The advanced industrialized states of the Marxist-Leninist "Second World" provided the twentieth century's most obvious examples. In these states, what we can term (following Pope John Paul II) the "interior freedom" of the human person was systematically violated.

3. This innate human quest for meaning and value, which is the basic dynamic of the "interior freedom" of the human person, is the end or object of that "human right" which we refer to as the "right of religious freedom," or "freedom of conscience."

Religious freedom or freedom of conscience is not a "grant" from the state or from society. Human beings are to enjoy the free and unfettered pursuit of truth simply because they are human beings, and because the denial of that pursuit is, in the deepest sense of the term, "inhuman." When we speak of the "right" of religious freedom or freedom of conscience, we are referring to the juridical expression of this basic claim about the essential core and dynamic of human personhood.

4. Thus religious freedom or freedom of conscience is the most fundamental of human rights.

It is the most fundamental because it is the right that corresponds to man's most fundamentally human dimension. For a state to refuse to honor religious freedom or freedom of conscience does not mean merely that its citizens lack one of the many goods in life; it means that the very structure of their being has been violated.

5. The right of religious freedom was defined with precision by Dignitatis Humanae Personae, the Second Vatican Council's Declaration on Religious Freedom, as follows: "The human person has a right to religious freedom. This freedom means that all men are to be immune from coercion on the part of individuals or of social groups and of any human power, in such wise that in matters religious no one is to be forced to act in a manner contrary to his beliefs. Nor is anyone to be restrained from acting in accordance with his own beliefs, whether privately or publicly, whether alone or in association with others, within due limits." [1]

This definition contains several important claims. First, it defines religious freedom as an issue involving the essence of the human person. Second, it acknowledges the privileges of conscience both for religious believers and for non-believers; religious belief is not coerced belief, nor should religious belief involve civil penalties for believers. Third, religious belief (or unbelief) is a public matter; men are to be free to act on their conscientious convictions, provided, as the Council later put it, "that the just requirements of public order are observed." Fourth, the right of religious freedom involves a concomitant obligation to pursue the truth, and a civic responsibility to see that society is structured such that truth can be publicly pursued.

The right of religious freedom therefore involves, of its very nature, both the right to the public profession of religious conviction, individually and in community, and immunity from coerced public religious profession or practice. This means that to argue publicly for or against religious conviction; to celebrate publicly, or abstain from celebrating, religious conviction; to transmit religious belief to one's children, or to keep them from such instruction; to establish organizations and institutions (educational, charitable, social-service) that are expressions of religious conviction— these are matters of individual conscientious decision, or of the decision of communities that form around matters of conviction. They are not to be subject to state policy or social coercion in any form, consonant with the minimum requirements of public order.

6. *Religious freedom or freedom of conscience can thus be considered a "pre-political" human right: religious freedom or freedom of conscience is the condition for the possibility of a polis that is structured in accordance with the inherent human dignity of its citizens.*

The right of religious freedom or freedom of conscience entails an obligation to seek the truth. If that right is not to be what Madison called a "parchment barrier," its observance requires that society be structured in such a way that all persons can engage in a depoliticized (i.e., non-coercive) search for truth, both privately and publicly, so that the rights of conscience are protected for all.

Here is where the "interior" meaning of religious freedom or freedom of conscience touches the "public" meaning.

THE PUBLIC MEANING OF
RELIGIOUS FREEDOM

7. *The right of religious freedom establishes a barrier or distinction between the person and the state that is essential in any just polity.*

While the right of religious freedom, in one form or another, has been asserted for centuries, it has been most forcefully claimed, and codified in international law, in this century of totalitarianism. Control of all aspects of human life is the declared intention of totalitarian states, as Hannah Arendt, Jeane Kirkpatrick, and others argued in distinguishing totalitarianism from traditional despotism or "authoritarianism." Conversely, the right of religious freedom declares that at the center of the human person is an inviolable sanctuary of conscience, a *sanctum sanctorum*, into which the coercive power of the state may not tread. States that do so tread are oppressors in the most fundamental sense. Religious conviction— or, more broadly, conscientious conviction that appeals to genuinely transcendent norms (as in the case of, say, non-believer Sidney Hook)—establishes the penultimacy of the political, because it gives public expression to what Peter Berger has called the "transcendent intentionality" of the human person.

8. The right of religious freedom is a crucial component in establishing the distinction between "society" and the "state" that is fundamental to the democratic project.

While the right of religious freedom or freedom of conscience can be observed in a modern authoritarian state (e.g., the Philippines of Ferdinand Marcos), the empirical fact is that religious freedom is most successfully safeguarded in democracies. That is because democracies are founded upon the concept of free persons constituting a free people under a limited state. Modern democratic theory and practice has multiple and complex roots: the English, Scottish, and French Enlightenments; Puritan moral intuitions ("The smallest he that is in England hath a life to lead as much as the greatest he," as Colonel Rainborough put it); Christian medieval political theory (with its notion of the people's inherent sense of justice, and its claim that the good prince rules by consent rather than by sheer coercion); classic Greek political philosophy and Roman law. However we weight these influences, though, democracy, in theory and in practice, rests upon the distinction between society and the state; upon the claim that society is prior to the state; and upon the understanding that the state exists to serve society, not the other way around. Social institutions, then, have a logical, historical, and even "ontological" priority over the institutions of government.

Among the social institutions that have most persistently claimed this priority in the West are religious institutions, and specifically the Christian Church. When Pope Gelasius I informed the Byzantine Emperor Anastasius I in A.D. 494 that "two there are, august emperor, by which this world is ruled on title of original and sovereign right—the consecrated authority of the priesthood and the royal power," he was rejecting any monistic (or, in modern times, "totalitarian") view of human society and polity. Gelasius I would not, of course, have argued the case for religious freedom on the personalist grounds suggested above; and his successors in the Christian community, Catholic and Protestant, were to honor this basic distinction more often in the breach than in the observance. But in this "Gelasian tradition" we may find, in ancient form, the basis of a rejection of totalitarian claims and, conversely, the root of those political understandings that eventually gave birth in the West to the democratic project.

9. *The priority of religious freedom in any meaningful scheme of "human rights" has been empirically confirmed, in modern times, by the totalitarian attack on religious belief and practice.*

It is not hard to see why totalitarian regimes—and particularly Leninist totalitarian regimes—put such ferocious efforts into the oppression of religious believers and institutions. Lenin understood, in a way that Marx did not, that religion threatened the very heart of the totalitarian project of constructing the "new man." The function of ideology in the totalitarian state was to make possible a thoroughgoing social control, a perverted anti-transcendence that would replace the transcendent horizon against which the society had once lived. The hammer and sickle constituted a crippled cross.

Paul Johnson, in *Modern Times*, captured this dimension of the Leninist enterprise well:

Religion was important to [Lenin] in the sense that he hated it. Unlike Marx, who despised it and treated it as marginal, Lenin saw it as a powerful and ubiquitous enemy. . . . "There can be nothing more abominable," he wrote, "than religion." From the start he created an enormous academic propaganda machine against religion. . . . Lenin had no feelings about corrupt priests, because they were easily beaten. The men he really feared and hated, and later persecuted, were the saints. The purer the religion, the more dangerous. . . . The clergy most in need of suppression were not those committed to the defense of exploitation but those who expressed their solidarity with the proletariat and the peasants. It was as though he recognized in the true man of God the same zeal and spirit which animated himself, and wished to expropriate it and enlist it in his own cause.[2]

Lenin's approach to religion was refined by his self-proclaimed heirs; the most popular instrument among those with Leninist ambitions in recent years seems not to have been a frontal assault on religious institutions so much as the establishment of parallel pseudo-religious institutions under state control (e.g., the *Pacem in Terris* organization in Czechoslovakia; the "popular church" in Nicaragua). But whether their tactics are direct or indirect, brutal or subtle, totalitarians seem to understand intuitively the priority of religious freedom, and the inevitable conflict between that freedom and their own designs for political power. For the state that honors the right of religious freedom or freedom of conscience is the state that acknowledges its own limits.

10. Democracies protect religious freedom, yet the relationship also cuts the other way: religious freedom is a fundamental guarantor of democracy.

This can be argued in two ways. First, the right of religious freedom or freedom of conscience, asserted in theory and observed in practice, helps create the conditions for addressing the threat of a Jacobin tyranny of the majority, or what some have called "totalitarian democracy." For the right of religious freedom is asserted against democratic majorities who would use coercion in matters of fundamental conscientious conviction just as much as it is asserted against the claims of true totalitarians. To the degree that religious freedom or freedom of conscience is observed in practice, and not merely bowed to in public rhetoric, the threat of Jacobinism is correspondingly diminished.

Thus democracies must tread with extreme care in deciding public policy issues that involve fundamental religious or moral convictions, as in the American debates over conscientious objection to military service or compulsory education for Amish children. The requirements of public order are of course a limiting factor; but in determining what religious practices gravely threaten civil unity or peace, a democracy should draw the boundaries as widely as possible—not only on humanitarian grounds but to honor the commitments that are the basic building-blocks of democratic political culture.

Religious freedom is also a guarantor of democracy in that the free expression of religious conviction and the moral understandings that flow therefrom in public debate over the right ordering of society address what Peter Berger has called the "serendipity" of liberty. Democracy is never a given, and democratic politics are not a matter of procedure alone. The democratic experiment—and democracy is always an experiment, a never-to-be-completed test of the capacity of human beings for self-government—requires certain habits (virtues) and attitudes as well as the more familiar ensemble of democratic procedures, such as separation of powers, election by secret ballot, legal protection for defeated political parties or candidates, and universal enfranchisement. The state itself has a measure of responsibility for inculcating democratic values and attitudes, as was well argued in the impressive statement "Education for Democracy," issued by the American Federation of Teachers in 1987. But experience suggests that democratic habits or virtues are most effectively nurtured by the "prior" institutions of society, particularly the family and religious institutions.

This seems to be the case in contemporary America, where democratic habits and commitments are intimately related to Jewish and Christian religious convictions as transmitted by parents and by religious institutions; the warrants that the majority of Americans cite in support of democracy have Judeo-Christian, not Enlightenment-philosophical, roots, as Richard John Neuhaus argued in *The Naked Public Square*. Religious freedom, at least as exercised in the United States and other Western democracies, seems to nurture political commitments that insure that the life of liberty and its expression in free institutions of governance is less than "serendipitous," and is in fact deeply grounded in the convictions of the people in whose name democratic political leaders claim to exercise authority.

11. The right relationship between religious freedom and the democratic project is best achieved in practice when there is no state "establishment" of religion.

It is true that the right of religious freedom or freedom of conscience is honored in democratic societies with established or "state" religious institutions, such as the United Kingdom. But there are two reasons to be concerned about this way of arranging the relationship between religious and political affairs.

First, religious institutions tend to weaken and atrophy when they are "kept" institutions. The vigor of the Roman Catholic Church in Poland, or, indeed, the vigor of Catholicism and other religious bodies under "disestablishment" in the United States, may be contrasted to the sclerotic condition of the Church of England, or to the moribund state of official Lutheranism in Scandinavia. The latter situations have many causes, but it seems unlikely that there is no causal connection between "establishment" and ecclesiastical senescence. Contrast also the weakened situation of those non-established Christian communities in Western Europe whose clergy nonetheless receive state salaries to the vigorous life of Christian communities in Africa or Latin America. Disestablishment is good for religion, as well as being more congruent with religious freedom in both its "private" and "public" meanings.

Disestablishment is also good for democracy. Establishment blurs, unnecessarily, the boundaries between state and society. And as these boundaries are an important element in democratic theory and practice, to blur them is to weaken the democratic project. The desacralizing of politics is an important political corollary of the right of religious freedom as well as a conceptual building-block of democratic theory and practice. When politics enters the sanctuary and political leaders exercise specific functions within religious institutions, politics is no longer seen as penultimate, and is made to carry a weight it cannot bear without lapsing into undesirable forms of coercion. Thus prime ministers who appoint bishops do damage to their own office as well as to the office of bishop.

Disestablishment ought to serve the end of the free exercise of religion, as Richard Neuhaus and others have argued. Would American constitutional theory and Supreme Court jurisprudence be in a less chaotic condition today had the Framers added a word to the First Amendment: "Congress shall make no law providing for an establishment of religion, or *otherwise* prohibiting the free exercise thereof"? The specific point is moot, of course, but the larger point remains: disestablishment is to the advantage of both church and state, to the cause of religious freedom as well as to the functioning of democratic polities.

Disestablishment does not, however, require utter separation between state institutions and religious institutions. Nor does it require—contrary to the claims of People for the American Way— that religiously based values be barred from public debate over the right ordering of society. In the pursuit of a recognized social good and public obligation (such as the education of children or the care of the elderly or orphaned), it makes no *essential* difference either to religious freedom or to democracy if public funds to achieve that good are channeled through religiously based institutions. (The effect of such funding on the charitable instincts of religious individuals and institutions is another matter.) Nor should disestablishment be taken to mean that religiously based values are ipso facto ruled out of bounds in public policy discourse. (The prudential wisdom of appeal to religious warrants in a pluralistic society is a different issue.) Here, however, we get in deep waters that are beyond the scope of this essay; for elaboration of the argument congruent with the one sketched here, readers may consult Neuhaus's *The Naked Public Square*.

THE PRIORITY OF RELIGIOUS FREEDOM IN THE THOUGHT OF JOHN PAUL II

The vigorous role played by the Roman Catholic Church in recent years as a principled advocate for the right of religious freedom or freedom of conscience is a notable development. I say "notable," because throughout the modern period, the magisterium of the Church held to the "thesis/hypothesis" view of church/state issues. In that view, as expounded most forcefully in the 1940s and 1950s by the late Cardinal Alfredo Ottaviani, the "thesis," or preferred arrangement, was the confessional state in which the Catholic Church would have not only cultural pride of place but also the active support of the civil authorities; Francoist Spain was one expression of this arrangement. Against it, the Church would tolerate, by reason of historical necessity, the "hypothesis" arrangement of a confessionally neutral state (as in the United States), or the establishment of another Christian faith by state authorities (e.g., in the United Kingdom or Sweden). But it was understood that one public task of the Church, under a "hypothesis" arrangement, was to work for the day when the "thesis" would prevail. In simplest form, the moral claim undergirding Ottaviani's formula was that "error has no rights," while its ecclesiological basis was the argument that the Catholic Church was the one and only true Church of Christ.

The challenge to Ottaviani's view mounted by the American Jesuit John Courtney Murray in the late 1940s and early 1950s eventually prevailed at the Second Vatican Council. In its original form, Murray's challenge drew on and extended the late-nineteenth-century church/state theory of Pope Leo XIII. The key shift was from Ottaviani's purely juridical view of "rights" to Murray's more personalist framing of the issue. The question, Murray argued, was not whether "error" has "rights." *Persons* have rights (and duties), and the right of religious freedom or freedom of conscience is among the foremost of these.

This was the teaching adopted by Vatican II in *Dignitatis Humanae Personae*, the Declaration on Religious Freedom. The Declaration dealt with what I have called the "interior meaning" of religious freedom, the right of persons to be free from the coercive power of the state in matters of conscientious conviction. But the Council did not devote significant attention to the "public meaning" of religious freedom, i.e., religious freedom as a right that creates the possibility for just governance in a rightly ordered society. This further development of the Catholic position has been undertaken by Pope John Paul II since his election in 1978.

The experience of the Church in the United States helped shape Murray's transformation of Catholic church/state theory such that the Council could adopt *Dignitatis Humanae Personae*. So, too, has John Paul II's experience of the Church in Poland under the heel of the two great totalitarian powers of the twentieth century shaped the most recent evolution of the Catholic argument on behalf of religious freedom. But John Paul's defense of that freedom begins, not with history or with political theory, and still less with denominational or institutional special pleading, but with that phenomenology of the human person that is so central to his thought.

The pope begins with a basic anthropological definition: "Man . . . is a person, that is to say a subjective being capable of acting in a planned and rational way, capable of deciding about himself and with a tendency to self-realization."[3] The pope then analyzes the threat to the integrity of the human person posed by the violation of the right of religious freedom today:

> Man rightly fears falling victim to an oppression that will deprive him of his interior freedom, of the possibility of expressing the truth of which he is convinced, of the faith that he professes, of the ability to obey the voice of conscience that tells him the right path to follow. The technical means at the disposal of modern society conceal within themselves not only the possibility of a "peaceful" subjugation of individuals, of environments, of entire societies and of nations, that for one reason or another might prove inconvenient for those who possess the necessary means and are ready to use them without scruple. . . . Together with the biological threat, therefore, there is a growing awareness of yet another threat, even more destructive of what is essentially human, what is intimately bound up with the dignity of the human person and his or her right to truth and freedom.[4]

John Paul's description of the "interior meaning" of religious freedom then leads him to the "public meaning" of this right. And here is where the pope expands the Council's discussion in *Dignitatis Humanae Personae*:

> The rights of power can only be understood on the basis of respect for the objective and inviolable rights of man. The common good that authority in the State serves is brought to full realization only when all citizens are sure of their rights. The lack of this leads to the dissolution of society, opposition by citizens to authority, or a situation of oppression, intimidation, violence, and terrorism, of which many examples have been provided by the totalitarianism of this century. Thus the principle of human rights is of profound concern to the area of social justice and is the measure by which it can be tested in the life of

political bodies. . . . These rights are reckoned to include the right of religious freedom together with the right of freedom of conscience. . . . Certainly the curtailment of the religious freedom of individuals and communities is not only a painful experience but it is above all an attack on man's dignity, independently of the religion professed or of the concept of the world which these individuals or communities have. The curtailment and violation of religious freedom are in contrast with man's dignity and his objective rights. . . . [They are] a radical unjustice to what is particularly deep within man, what is authentically human.[5]

The pope's discussion of the relation between religious freedom and the just society was further extended in the "Instruction on Christian Freedom and Liberation" issued by the Congregation for the Doctrine of the Faith in March 1986. The instruction was, in part, a response to those currents in the theologies of liberation that would subordinate the right of religious freedom to other putative social, economic, or political goods. In a document issued with the pope's personal authority, the Congregation declared:

There can only be authentic development in a social and political system which respects freedoms and fosters them through the participation of everyone. This participation can take many forms; it is necessary in order to guarantee the proper pluralism in institutions and in social initiatives. It ensures, notably by the real separation between the powers of the State, the exercise of human rights, also protecting them against possible abuses on the part of the public powers. No one can be excluded from this participation in social and political life for reasons of sex, race, color, social condition, language, or religion. . . . When the political authorities regulate the exercise of freedoms, they cannot use the pretext of the demands of public order and security in order to curtail those freedoms systematically. Nor can the alleged principle of national security, or a narrowly economic outlook, or a totalitarian concept of social life, prevail over the value of freedom and its right.[6]

Thus the pope's claim that "religious freedom . . . is the basis of all other freedoms and is inseparably tied to them all by reason of that very dignity which is the human person" (Letter to United Nations Secretary General Waldheim, 2 December 1978) addresses both the "interior" and the "public" meaning of the right of religious freedom or freedom of conscience. The pope believes, as Father James V. Schall, S.J., has put it, that "the state is legally incompetent at man's deepest levels, in his spirit, but . . . it can and ought to recognize the importance of religious values for the state's own progress."[7] Thus the pope could address the ambassador of Senegal in these terms:

> Tolerance and peace among the disciples of the great religious confessions are facilitated by the institutions of your country. With regard to these religious confessions, the state keeps the distance which permits the necessary impartiality and the normal distinction between political interest and religious matters. But this distinction is not indifference: the state knows how to mark its esteem for spiritual values and encourage, with justice, the services that religious communities render to the population in the field of education and medical care.[8]

Religious freedom is not, for John Paul II, a matter of mere assertion. Religious freedom requires, and creates the conditions for, social and political arrangements in which the inviolable rights of the person are respected, a (profoundly anti-totalitarian) distinction between "society" and "state" is constitutionally maintained, and the state thus has limited powers. But the Church, according to the pope, seeks religious freedom not just for the sake of its own evangelical mission but for the good of society as a whole:

> Since it is the servant of humanity, the Church will always be disposed to collaborate in the promotion of justice, peace, and human dignity by means of the active participation of its members in common initiatives, by proclaiming incessantly that all human beings are made in the image and likeness of God and are, hence, endowed with equal dignity and rights.[9]

In the thought of John Paul II, therefore, says Schall, "religious liberty . . . is both an avenue whereby higher motivations can exist in the public order, and a limit [on] politics so that man's higher truth and destiny can be presented and achieved at a depth that is not properly external or political. John Paul has . . . bridged the perplexing question of how religion can be not of this world and yet at the same time confronted by earthly realities, without destroying the dignity and value of public life and politics. In this he has made a unique contribution to the history of the idea of freedom by placing it directly in the line of the whole truth about man."[10]

The truth about man includes moral judgments about the right ordering of society, as the pope made clear while en route to South America in 1987. Asked by a reporter on his plane whether he would not be meddling in politics during his visit to Chile, the pope responded: "Yes, yes, I am not the evangelizer of democracy, I am the evangelizer of the Gospel. To the Gospel message, of course, belong all the problems of human rights, and if democracy means human rights it also belongs to the message of the Church."[11]

The sequence within this brief statement is instructive. The Church is the Church, not a political lobby ("I am the evangelizer of the Gospel"). But the Church is neither privatistic nor quietistic ("to the Gospel message, of course, belong all the problems of human rights"). And the Church has come to understand that the mere assertion of human rights is insufficient; it must address also the question of institutions of freedom ("and if democracy means human rights it also belongs to the message of the Church"). Religious conviction leads to moral norms, which then lead to issues of the right-ordering of social and political institutions. To say "religious freedom" is to say something about democracy, or, at a minimum, about pre-democratic arrangements in which basic human rights are honored and the distinction between society and state maintained. The relevance of these concepts to modern political life is obvious from the pope's direct and indirect role in the creation of *Solidarnosc* in Poland, and from the role the Church played in many of the democratic revolutions of the late 1980s.

Finally, John Paul II has linked religious freedom or freedom of conscience to the pursuit of peace in world affairs. In an address to the United Nations General Assembly in 1979, he said,

> Man can be wounded in his inner relationship with truth, in his conscience, in his most personal belief, in his view of the world, in his religious faith, and in the sphere of what are known as civil liberties. . . . For centuries the thrust of civilization has been in

one direction: that of giving the life of individual political societies a form in which there can be fully safeguarded the objective rights of the spirit, of human conscience, and of human creativity, including man's relationship with God. . . .

Besides the acceptance of legal formulas safeguarding the principle of the freedom of the human spirit, such as freedom of thought and expression, religious freedom, and freedom of conscience, structures of social life often exist in which the practical exercise of these freedoms condemns man, in fact if not formally, to become a second-class or third-class citizen, to see compromised his chances of social advancement, his professional career, or his access to certain posts of responsibility, and to lose even the possibility of educating his children freely. It is a question of the highest importance that in internal social life, as well as in international life, all human beings in every nation and country should be able to enjoy effectively their full rights under any regime or system.

Only the safeguarding of this real completeness of rights for every human being without discrimination can ensure peace at its very roots.[12]

The religious discussion of religious freedom as the first human right has by no means been limited to the Roman Catholic Church; in one sense, we can say that the Catholic magisterium is catching up with Roger Williams. But the doctrine of religious freedom sketched by John Paul II may be of particular interest: first, because of the historical transition it bespeaks in Catholic social theory; second, because of the size and impact of the Church as an international actor; third, because the pope's fundamental argument on behalf of religious freedom is cast, not in denominationally specific terms, but in a language accessible to all men of good will, religious or not; and fourth, because of the pope's linkage between religious freedom and certain political-institutional arrangements, and between religious freedom and peace. Thus the theory of religious freedom set forth by John Paul II speaks tellingly to pluralistic societies like the United States, as well as, of course to our luxuriantly plural world.

THE TEMPTATIONS OF RELIGIOUS FREEDOM

In a legendary conference he gave to a generation of American Jesuits during pre-ordination retreats, John Courtney Murray used

to warn against the "temptations of the vows." The vow of obedience could be a temptation to intellectual sloth, the vow of chastity,
to aridity in human relationships, the vow of poverty, to irrespon-
sibility in the use of material goods. Beware, Murray warned, the
temptations of the vows.

The good of religious freedom, too, involves social and political
temptations. In developed democracies, for example, it can too
blithely be assumed that the institutionalization of religious freedom has solved all the knotty problems of how moral norms relate
to social structures or public policy.

If the "right of religious freedom" is reduced to an ensemble of
constitutional and legal procedures—if complacency over our legal
protection of the "private meaning" of this right leads us to ignore
its "public meaning"—then we have traduced the right of religious
freedom. To put it another way, if the right of religious freedom is
reduced, in public understanding, to a matter of individual "taste,"
so that the moral norms attendant on religious truth claims are
deemed merely matters of "preference," we will soon find ourselves
in a situation in which public moral discourse is replaced by public
moral emoting—a situation like that described by Alasdair Mac-
Intyre in *After Virtue*, in which we can no longer say "You *ought*
to . . . " in public life. And if democratic governance is a never-
finished experiment testing the human capacity for self-rule, the
reduction of the right of religious freedom to its "interior meaning"
alone can produce a society that is morally and spiritually empty at
its core.

The Church, in defending religious freedom, may also be
tempted to feel satisfied when its own position as an institution
independent of governmental control is secure. But if the "public
meaning" of religious freedom is taken seriously, religious communities will commit themselves to helping create or strengthen
those many mediating institutions that make up "civil society,"
institutions whose health and well-being are essential to democratic
governance. Or, as a young Polish Catholic sociologist put it in the
wake of the revolution of 1989, the Church has an obligation to
help break, for the sake of civil society, its "monopoly on good-
ness." The Catholic Church in Poland and Czechoslovakia has
shown dramatically that the human rights concerns of the religious

community are not fully met merely because the community's own functioning is legally protected.

Finally, there is what we might call a "doctrinal" temptation in the right of religious freedom. Religious belief involves truth claims about matters of ultimate consequence. The "procedures" of religious freedom as worked out in a multi-denominational society like the United States can take the edge off those claims. John Murray Cuddihy's *No Offense: Civil Religion and Protestant Taste*[13] may be taken as the most curmudgeonly recent exploration of this problem. Does the right of religious freedom necessarily yield a "civil religion of civility" in which religious truth claims are muted and ultimately dissolved out of a concern for showing "good taste"? Is the net result a least-common-denominator religiosity, a religion-of-the-American-way-of-life? So Cuddihy argues (echoing Will Herberg a generation before), and Stanley Hauerwas inclines to agree, although he might reject the qualifier "necessarily."[14]

On the other side of the debate, Richard Neuhaus and others have argued that it is precisely the kinds of social and political arrangements we enjoy in the United States that make it possible to engage religious differences forthrightly—in both their internal-doctrinal and public-policy respects—within the bond of a democratic civility that eventually sharpens theological understanding. Neuhaus and those on his side of the debate would recognize the temptation that Cuddihy and Hauerwas warn against; but they would see it as precisely that, a temptation, and not a necessary concomitant of the right and practice of religious freedom.

That debate seems likely to continue, as indeed it should. For its continuation is a compliment to, and a vindication of, both the interior and the public meaning of the right of religious freedom.

2

Catholicism and Democracy:
The Other Twentieth-Century
Revolution

In a conversation early in the 1980s, Sir Michael Howard, the Regius professor of modern history at Oxford, suggested that there had been two great revolutions in the twentieth century. The first took place when Lenin's Bolsheviks expropriated the Russian people's revolution in November 1917. The second was going on even as we spoke: the transformation of the Roman Catholic Church from a bastion of the *ancien régime* into perhaps the world's foremost institutional defender of human rights. It was a fascinating reading of the history of our century. One also sensed, in Sir Michael's story, just the slightest hint of an element of surprise: fancy that—the Vatican as defender of the rights of man!

There are, to be sure, reasons to be surprised by the contemporary Vatican's aggressive defense of human rights, and by Pope John Paul II's endorsement of democracy as the form of government that best coheres with the Church's vision of "integral human development." In the worlds of political power, those surprised would have to include the late Leonid Brezhnev (puzzled by the concurrent rise of *Solidarnosc* and the election of a Polish pope), Ferdinand Marcos, Augusto Pinochet, and the leaders of the Czechoslovak Communist party. On the other hand, key themes in classic Catholic social ethics—personalism, the common good, and the principle of subsidiarity—seem not merely congruent with democracy but pointed positively toward the evolution of liberal democratic forms of governance.

25

That, of course, would come as news indeed to Popes Gregory XVI and Pius IX, whose attitudes toward liberal democracy were decidedly chilly. What has happened between the mid-nineteenth century and now, between an official Catholic skepticism about democracy that bordered on hostility, and a Catholic endorsement of democracy that not only threatens tyrants but actually helps to topple them?

THE MID-NINETEENTH-CENTURY ARGUMENT

The hostility of official Roman Catholicism's papal magisterium to the liberal concepts of the rights of man as defined in the creed of the French Revolution, and to the liberal democratic state, is well known to all students of the period. It is neatly encapsulated in that last of the condemned propositions in Pius IX's 1864 *Syllabus of Errors*, viz., that "the Roman Pontiff can and should reconcile himself to and agree with progress, liberalism, and modern civilization." What is perhaps less well known is that Pius IX, Giovanni Maria Mastai-Ferretti, was elected in 1846 as a reforming pope with a more tolerant attitude toward modern thought and institutions than his predecessor, Gregory XVI (1831–46), who, in the 1832 and 1834 encyclicals *Mirari Vos* and *Singulari Nos*, had flatly condemned liberalism (including "this false and absurd maxim, or better this madness, that everyone should have and practice freedom of conscience") as essentially irreligious.[1] In any case, events—particularly the Italian *Risorgimento*, whose liberal anti-clerical leadership made no pretense about its intention to dislodge traditional church authority throughout Italy—hardened Pius IX in his views such that, by the time of the First Vatican Council (1869–70), the pope who had been elected twenty-three years earlier as something of a reformer had become, throughout the world, the very symbol of intransigent resistance to the ideas and institutions of modernity.[2]

While there were undoubtedly personal factors involved in the retrenchment strategy of Pius IX, it seems far more fruitful to focus on the substantive reasons why official Catholicism found itself in resistance to the liberal project in the nineteenth century. At least four suggest themselves to this observer.

The Jacobin Spirit

First, one should not discount the enduring effects of the shock that the French Revolution sent through European Catholicism—a shock of perhaps greater intensity than any other the Church had absorbed since the Reformation. There was, to be sure, the crazed bloodiness of the Terror itself. But beyond that, and beyond even Napoleon's persecution of Pope Pius VII, the leadership of Roman Catholicism saw the lingering specter of Jacobinism as an ideological force that threatened the very foundations of European civilization.[3]

That civilization, in its public aspects, had been rooted in the notion that states, as well as individual men, were accountable to transcendent moral norms (generally held to be revealed by a God who was sovereign over states as well as over individuals). By its defiant insistence on the autonomous reason of man as the first, and indeed only, principle of political organization, Jacobinism threatened not simply the position of the Church as mediator between the sovereign God and his creatures. The anti-clerical laicism imbedded in Jacobinism was a problem, to be sure. But the greater threat, in the Church's view, was that the Jacobin spirit inevitably led to the implosion of civilization and its consequent collapse into mobocracy, or what J. R. Talmon has called totalitarian democracy.[4]

Thus a damning equation hardened in the minds of a church leadership that had long identified, not merely its institutional prerogatives, but civilization itself with the moral understandings that (in however attenuated a form) underlay the structures of the *ancien régime*: liberalism = Jacobinism = (anti-clericalism + The Terror + anarchy). Discriminating or not, fair or not, the brush of Robespierre tarred the revolutionaries of 1848, the leaders of the Italian *Risorgimento* (Cavour, Mazzini, Garibaldi, and the like), and in fact the entire liberal project in Europe.[5]

Centralization of the Church

The second factor that colored the mid-nineteenth-century Church's appraisal of liberalism and democracy was the Church's own internal situation. The answer that Roman Catholicism devised to the political threat posed by the rise of post-monarchical states in Europe and to the advance of liberal ideas was centralization: the radical concentration of effective authority over virtually all matters, great and small, in the person (and, of course, staff) of the Roman pontiff. The pope would be the sole judge of orthodoxy and orthopraxis; the pope would manage the Church's affairs with sovereign states through an expanding network of papal diplomats, concordat arrangements, and so forth. *Ubi Petrus, ibi ecclesia* ("Where there is Peter, there is the Church") is an ancient theological maxim. But it was given new breadth in the nineteenth century in response to the ideological (and, indeed, physical) threats posed by the forces of what the *Syllabus* called "progress, liberalism, and modern civilization."

There is, of course, an irony, here: the Church's answer to the threat of "progress, liberalism, and modern civilization" was to adopt a quintessentially modern structure, i.e., one that was highly centralized and bureaucratically controlled. Be that irony as it may, though, the new emphasis on centralized authority, coupled with the traditional understanding of the divinely given prerogatives of the Roman pontiff, and further complicated by the dependence of the Papal States (pre-1870) on European monarchs for physical security, created a situation in which the Church's leadership was rather unlikely to feel much of an affinity with liberal democracy. In terms of the sociology of knowledge, the conditions-for-the-possibility of a Roman pontiff's looking with much favor on liberal democracy were not, to put it mildly, in place.

A Threatening Package

In the third place, and as if the above were not enough barriers to rapprochement, liberalism in the latter part of the nineteenth century was widely (and not altogether inaccurately) perceived in Vatican circles as a package deal that included Darwinism, which seemed to threaten the distinctiveness of human beings in creation; "higher criticism" or the "historical-critical method," which seemed to challenge the integrity of the Bible and its status as the revealed Word of God; and socialism, which seemed to threaten the Church's traditional teaching on the right of private property. To these perceived threats in the order of ideas must be added the physical threat of revolutionary Marxism as it showed itself in, say, the 1870 Paris Commune.

The most fundamental reason for the Church's resistance to the liberal democratic project in the nineteenth century should not, however, be located on this institutional/ideological axis. The institutional threats noted above were real, in both corporate and personal terms, and they did act as a kind of filter through which ideas and events were, in some cases, misperceived. But beneath it all lay, I believe, an evangelical concern.

The Road to Indifference

Rightly or wrongly, the central leadership of nineteenth-century Roman Catholicism truly believed that religious liberty—a key plank in the platform of liberal democracy—would inevitably lead to religious indifference and, given the right circumstances, to hostility toward religion on the part of governments. The secularization of Western Europe in the nineteenth century was a complicated business,[6] and it would be a grave historical error to attribute it solely (or even primarily) to the collapse of the old altar-and-throne arrangements that had obtained since the Peace of Westphalia ended the European wars of religion in 1648. On the other hand, and from the Vatican's point of view at that time, secularization proceeded apace with the collapse of those arrangements. Those of us with the luxury of hindsight should be perhaps less quick to dismiss as unfounded the inferences that were drawn. As for the breakdown of altar-and-throne eventually leading to governmental hostility toward religion, there was, at the beginning of the nineteenth century, the Napoleonic persecution of the Church; and after 1870 there was the pressing problem of the violently anti-clerical Third French Republic, in the face of which it was all too easy to read the historical record backwards, from the depredations of the Commune and the later anti-clericalism of the Third Republic to the *Declaration des Droits de L'Homme et du Citoyen*.

One cannot, in short, dismiss Roman resistance to the liberal democratic project as merely institutional self-interest. Some liberal democratic states put grave difficulties in the path of the Church's evangelical and sacramental mission, and larger conclusions, appropriate or otherwise, were shortly drawn.

On the other hand, it should also be conceded that the Roman authorities were slow to seize the opportunities presented by what might be called the Catholic Whig tradition, which looks to Thomas Aquinas for its inspiration and which had, in Lord Acton, a powerful spokesman in the mid- and late-nineteenth century. Given his largely negative views on the utility of the definition of papal infallibility at the First Vatican Council (itself, *inter alia*, an act of defiance against the epistemological spirit of the age), Acton was an unlikely broker of this tradition, which taught the possibility of genuine progress in history when that progress is mediated through rightly ordered public institutions holding themselves accountable to transcendent moral norms.

In any case, the Catholic Whig tradition, a revolutionary liberal tradition in its own right, if in sharp contrast to the Jacobinism with which the Vatican typically associated liberalism, would not have all that long to wait for its moment to arrive.

THE TURN TOWARD DEMOCRACY

What accounts for the shift in official Catholic teaching in the period 1864–1965, between the rejection of the modern constitutional state in the *Syllabus of Errors* and the Second Vatican Council's acceptance of the juridical state in its *Declaration on Religious Freedom*? Of the many factors in play, one strikes me as particularly important: the fact of America.

In the United States, the Church was confronted with a liberal society and liberal democratic state that were good for Roman Catholics. Religious liberty and the constitutional separation of church and state had led not to religious indifferentism but to a vibrant Catholicism that still, unlike its European counterparts, held the allegiance of the working class. Moreover, while anti-Catholicism was a fact of life in the United States,[7] the U.S. government had never come close to conducting an overt program of persecution on the basis of religious conviction.

The Gibbons Manifesto

This was somewhat difficult to handle for those in Rome who were still committed to a restoration of the *ancien régime*, or even those who were simply skeptical about the American experiment. A bold, public attempt to press the argument for religious liberty and liberal democracy in Rome itself took place on March 25, 1887, when the newly created Cardinal James Gibbons of Baltimore took possession of his titular Church of Santa Maria in Trastevere, and preached to his Roman congregation in these terms:

> Scarcely were the United States formed when Pius VI, of happy memory, established there the Catholic hierarchy and appointed the illustrious John Carroll first Bishop of Baltimore. This event, so important to us, occurred less than a hundred years ago. . . . Our Catholic community in those days numbered only a few thousand souls . . . served by the merest handful of priests. Thanks to the fructifying grace of God, the . . . seed then planted has grown to be a large tree, spreading its branches over the length and width of our fair land. . . . For their great progress under God and the fostering care of the Holy See *we are indebted in no small degree to the civil liberty we enjoy in our enlightened republic.*
>
> Our Holy Father, Leo XIII, in his luminous encyclical on the constitution of Christian States, declares that the Church is not committed to any particular form of civil government. She adapts to all; she leavens all with the sacred leaven of the Gospel. She has lived under absolute empires; she thrives under constitutional monarchies; she grows and expands under the free republic. She has often, indeed, been hampered in her divine mission and has had to struggle for a footing wherever despotism has cast its dark shadow . . . but in the genial air of liberty she blossoms like the rose!
>
> For myself, as a citizen of the United States, and without closing my eyes to our defects as a nation, I proclaim, with a deep sense of pride and gratitude, and in this great capital of Christendom, that I belong to a country where the civil government holds over us the aegis of its protection without interfering in the legitimate exercise of our sublime mission as ministers of the Gospel of Jesus Christ.
>
> Our country has liberty without license, authority without despotism. . . . But, while we are acknowledged to have a free government, we do not, perhaps, receive due credit for possessing also a strong government. Yes, our nation is strong, and her strength lies, under Providence, in the majesty and supremacy of

the law, in the loyalty of her citizens to that law, and in the affection of our people for their free institutions.[8]

Gibbons's proud assertions sound mild to our ears, but in their own day they were intended as a manifesto and a challenge, and were understood as such by celebrants and detractors alike. As Gerald Fogarty, S.J., puts it, "Here was the gauntlet of the benefit of American religious liberty thrown down by the new world to the old."[9]

Leo XIII: Toleration

Pope Leo XIII (1878–1903) was happy to acknowledge the practical benefits of the American arrangement in the American circumstance, but he was not yet prepared to concede the moral superiority of the liberal (i.e., confessionally neutral) state over the classic European arrangements. In his 1895 encyclical letter to the American hierarchy, *Longinqua Oceani*, Leo cautioned against any temptation to universalize the American experience and experiment:

> The Church amongst you, unopposed by the Constitution and government of your nation, fettered by no hostile legislation, protected against violence by the common laws and the impartiality of the tribunals, is free to live and act without hindrance. Yet, though all this is true, it would be very erroneous to draw the conclusion that in America is to be sought the type of the most desirable status of the Church, or that it would be universally lawful or expedient for State and Church to be, as in America, dissevered and divorced. The fact that Catholicity with you is in good condition, nay, is even enjoying a prosperous growth, is by all means to be attributed to the fecundity with which God has endowed his Church, in virtue of which unless men or circumstances interfere, she spontaneously expands and propagates herself; but she would bring forth more abundant fruits if, in addition to liberty, she enjoyed the favor of the laws and the patronage of the public authority.[10]

Thus the situation in the late nineteenth century: the American arrangement and the liberal democratic, confessionally neutral state it represents *tolerari potest* (could be tolerated). Indeed, the accomplishments of the Church under such a new arangement could be forthrightly and gratefully acknowledged. This was quite a step ahead of the rejectionist posture of Pius IX and the *Syllabus*. But we have yet to reach the stage at which the confessionally neutral state that acknowledges the right of religious liberty as an inalienable right of human beings as such, prior to their status as citizens, is preferred to a benign altar-and-throne (or altar-and-desk) arrangement.

Moving Beyond Toleration

The path to that more developed position, which is the basis of the contemporary Catholic rapprochement with liberal democracy, would be traversed over the next sixty years. The vigor of American Catholicism continued to play a role, by way of example, in insuring that the issue remained alive. The providential loss of the Papal States had a beneficial effect, also. Absent this direct political responsibility, popes from Leo XIII on were in a more advantageous position to consider, from a far less encumbered theological and practical position, the relative merits of various forms of modern governance.

As the nineteenth century gave way to the twentieth, other realities of modern life began to influence the Church's perspective. Among the most significant was the rise of totalitarianism, in both its Leninist and its fascist form, and the threat posed to Roman Catholicism by both of these demonic modern political movements. The Church was led, not only to look toward the democracies for protection, but also to look toward democracy itself as an antidote to the totalitarian temptation. This was particularly true in the immediate post–World War II period, when Vatican diplomacy, often working closely with U.S. diplomats and occupation forces, worked to strengthen Christian Democratic parties in Germany and Italy. In the Italian case, this represented a shift indeed, for Pope Pius XI (1922–39) had summarily ended the proto–Christian Democratic experiment led by Don Luigi Sturzo in the early twentieth century—with most unfortunate results.[11]

In any event, Christian Democracy, in theory and in practice, seemed to many Vatican minds (including that of Giovanni Battista

Montini, later Pope Paul VI) the best available alternative to either Leninist or fascist totalitarianism, in a world where even constitutional monarchy was clearly on the wane. Montini was influenced in this judgment by his regard for the philosophical work of the French neo-Thomist Jacques Maritain, whose *Christianity and Democracy*, written during the summer of 1942, became a kind of theoretical manifesto for the Christian Democratic movement.[12]

The Church's turn toward Christian Democracy was also facilitated by the decline of anti-clericalist bias among European liberals, and by the difference-in-kind between liberals and radicals that totalitarian persecution made horribly plain. The Vatican may still have had its differences with liberals, but after the ruthless persecution of Christianity under Lenin and Stalin, the Ukrainian terror famine, and the Holocaust, it was no longer possible even to suggest that modern radical dictators such as Stalin and Hitler were but exceptionally virulent forms of a general liberal virus. In the French situation, cooperative efforts during World War II between Catholic intellectuals and a few religious leaders, and the wider Resistance movement (with its secularist and Marxist leaderships), helped break down some of the stereotypes that had plagued life under the Third Republic.[13] In Italy, the tradition of Don Sturzo, incarnated in such major post-war figures as de Gasperi and Moro, could be reclaimed, just as in Germany Konrad Adenauer was able to tap the Christian Democratic tradition of the old Catholic Center party.[14]

In the post–World War II period, then, new facts of national and international life validated Gibbons's thesis beyond the borders of the United States, and created the sociological conditions for retrieving Pius VII's views on the compatibility of Catholicism and democracy.

Finally, and perhaps most significantly in terms of the history of ideas, the evolution of Catholic social teaching itself pushed the Church toward a more positive appraisal of liberal democracy. The key development here was Pius XI's emphasis on subsidiarity. This principle was central to the pope's teaching in *Quadragesimo Anno*, issued in 1931 for the fortieth anniversary of Leo XIII's groundbreaking social encyclical *Rerum Novarum*. The key passage in Pius XI's letter was the following:

It is true, as history clearly shows, that because of changed circumstances much that formerly was performed by small associations can now be accomplished only by larger ones. Nevertheless, it is a fixed and unchangeable principle, most basic in social philosophy, immoveable and unalterable, that, just as it is wrong to take away from individuals what they can accomplish by their own ability and effort and entrust it to a community, so it is an injury and at the same time both a serious evil and a disturbance of right order to assign to a larger and higher society what can be performed successfully by smaller and lower communities. The reason is that all social activity, of its very power and nature, should supply help [*subsidium*] to the members of the social body, but may never destroy or absorb them.

The state, then, should leave to these smaller groups the settlement of business and problems of minor importance, which would otherwise greatly distract it. Thus it will carry out with greater freedom, power, and success the tasks belonging to it alone, because it alone is qualified to perform them: directing, watching, stimulating, and restraining, as circumstances suggest or necessity demands. Let those in power, therefore, be convinced that the more faithfully this principle of subsidiary function is followed and a graded hierarchical order exists among the various associations, the greater also will be both social authority and social efficiency, and the happier and more prosperous too will be the condition of the commonwealth.[15]

Elements of Subsidiarity

As it has worked itself out in subsequent Catholic social teaching, the principle of subsidiarity consists of the following substantive elements:

1. The individual human person is both the source and the end of society. *Civitas propter cives, non cives propter civitatem*: the state exists for the benefit of its citizens, not the citizens for the state.

2. Yet the human person is "naturally" social, and can achieve the fullness of human development only in human communities. This is sometimes referred to, particularly in analyses of the writings of John Paul II, as the principle of solidarity.

3. The purpose of social relationships and human communities is to give help (*subsidium*) to individuals as they pursue, freely, their

obligation to work for their own human development. Thus the state or society should not, save in exceptional circumstances, replace or displace this individual self-responsibility; the society and the state provide conditions under which self-responsibility may be exercised.

4. There is a hierarchy of communities in human society; larger, "higher" communities are to provide help (*subsidium*), in the manner noted above, to smaller or "lower" communities.

5. *Positively*, the principle of subsidiarity means that all communities should encourage and enable (not merely permit) individuals to exercise their self-responsibility, and larger communities should do this for smaller communities. Put another way, decision-making responsibility in society should rest at the "lowest" possible level commensurate with the effective pursuit of the common good.[16]

6. *Negatively*, the principle means that communities must not deprive individuals, nor larger communities deprive smaller communities, of the opportunity to do what they can for themselves.

Subsidiarity, in other words, is a formal principle "by which to regulate competencies between individual and communities and between smaller and larger communities." Because it is a formal principle, its precise meaning "on the ground" will differ according to circumstances; because it is rooted in "the metaphysics of the person, it applies to the life of every society."[17]

There is both a historical and a substantive connection between the identification of the principle of subsidiarity and the Roman Catholic Church's increasingly positive appraisal of democracy in the mid-twentieth century. Historically, the very concept of subsidiarity was developed in the German Königswinterer Kreis, a group of Catholic intellectuals interested in questions of political economy, who deeply influenced both the author of *Quadragesimo Anno* (the Jesuit Oswald von Nell-Breuning) and the evolution of Christian Democracy in pre- and post-war Germany.[18]

The substantive connection was closely related to the historical connection. *Quadragesimo Anno* was written under the lengthening shadow of totalitarianism. If its predecessor encyclical, *Rerum Novarum*, had been written, at least in part, to warn against the dangers inherent in Manchesterian liberalism, *Quadragesimo Anno* was written in response to the threat posed by the overweening pretensions of the modern state.[19] Hence the importance of the principle of subsidiarity, which tried, *inter alia*, to set clear boundaries to state power.

The question then arises: Under modern circumstances, what form of governance is most likely to acknowledge, in practice as well as in principle or rhetoric, the limited role of the state, the moral and social importance of what Burke called the "small platoons," and the principle of *civitas propter cives*? A number of theoretical possibilities come to mind, but in actual historical practice, it is liberal democracies that best meet these moral criteria. This was not precisely what Pius XI, with his corporatist vision, had in mind in 1931, but it was certainly what Pope Pius XII (1939–58) had in mind by the mid-1940s. Pius XII was not a "global democrat," as a later generation of American paleoconservatives would say. But he did seem to think that democracy provided the best available modern form of government in the developed world.

VATICAN II ON CHURCH AND STATE

The proximate origins of what I have termed elsewhere the "Catholic human rights revolution,"[20] which led in turn to the Church's new appreciation for, and overt support of, the democratic revolution in world politics, should be located in the Second Vatican Council's *Declaration on Religious Freedom* (so aptly styled, in its Latin title, *Dignitatis Humanae Personae*), issued in 1965. The *Declaration* was itself a child of the American experience and experiment, and a brief sketch of that background is in order.

The chief intellectual architect of the Declaration was the U.S. Jesuit theologian John Courtney Murray. Beginning in the late 1940s, Murray conceived and orchestrated a creative extension of Catholic church/state theory. The official Roman position, when Murray first took up the topic, was precisely where Leo XIII had left it in *Longinqua Oceani*: the "thesis," or preferred arrangement, was the legal establishment of Catholicism on either the classic altar-and-throne or the modern Francoist model; the American arrangement, i.e., religious liberty for all in a confessionally neutral state, was a tolerable "hypothesis." Moreover, in a confessionally neutral state, the Church ought (according to the official position) to work for the day when it, too, would enjoy the benefits of state support.

The "thesis" arrangement, with its rejection of religious liberty as a fundamental human right, was grounded on the moral-theological maxim that "error has no rights," which meant, in public terms, that "erroneous" religious communities (such as the sundry forms of Protestantism in America) should not, under "ideal" circumstances, receive the tolerant (if tacit) blessing of the state. This view was defended by prominent American Catholic theologians like Joseph Clifford Fenton and Francis Connell, C.SS.R., of the Catholic University of America, and the *American Ecclesiastical Review*.[21]

Murray's challenge to this position, and his creative extension of Catholic church/state theory, involved a classically Murrayesque maneuver, i.e., the retrieval and development of a largely forgotten current in Catholic thought that antedated the altar-and-throne model. Murray found the *locus classicus* of this forgotten current in a letter to the Byzantine emperor Anastasius in 494, in which Pope Gelasius I had written, "Two there are, august emperor, by which this world is ruled on title of original and sovereign right—the consecrated authority of the priesthood and the royal power." As I have written elsewhere about this modest but crucial statement,

> This was not a radical "two kingdoms" construct so much as a declaration of independence for both Church and state. The Church's freedom to exercise its ministry of truth and charity was a limit on the powers of government; the state's lack of authority in matters spiritual "desacralized" politics and, by doing so, opened up the possibility of a politics of consent, in place of the politics of divine right or the politics of coercion. The Gelasian tradition frowned on a unitary Church/state system for the sake of the integrity of both religion and politics.[22]

After considerable theological and ecclesiastical-political maneuvering, Murray's Gelasian retrieval prevailed at Vatican II. Enriched by a personalist philosophical approach that taught that persons had rights, even if their opinions were erroneous, the Gelasian tradition was incorporated into the Declaration, with a palpable effect on the Church's subsequent attitude toward democracy.

Religious Freedom: The Interior Meaning

The connection here—between the definition of religious freedom as a fundamental human right and the affirmation of democratic forms of governance—has to do with the very nature of religious freedom itself, for religious freedom has both an "interior" meaning and a "public" meaning.

The interior meaning of religious freedom can be stated in these terms: Because human beings, as persons, have an innate capacity for thinking, doing, and choosing and an innate drive for meaning and value, freedom to pursue that quest for meaning and value, without coercion, is a fundamental requisite for a truly human life. This innate quest for meaning and value, which is the basic dynamic of what John Paul II has called the interior freedom of the human person, is the object or end of that human right which we call the right of religious freedom; the right of religious freedom, in other words, is the juridical expression of this basic claim about the constitutive elements and dynamic of human being in the world.

One can argue, then, that religious freedom—as the Council put it, the claim that "all men are to be immune from coercion on the part of individuals or of social groups and of any human power, in such wise that in matters religious no one is to be forced to act in a manner contrary to his beliefs"[23]—is the most fundamental of human rights, because it is the claim that corresponds to the most radically human dimension of human being in the world.

Religious Freedom: The Public Meaning

This brings us to the public meaning of religious freedom. On the personalist analysis above, religious freedom can be considered a pre-political human right: it is the condition for the possibility of a *polis* structured in accordance with the inherent human dignity of the persons who are its citizens. Thus the right of religious freedom establishes a fundamental barrier between the person and the state that is essential to a just *polis*. The state is not omnicompetent, and one of the reasons we know this is that the right of religious freedom is the juridical expression of the pre-political fact that there is a *sanctum sanctorum* within every human person wherein coercive power (most especially including coercive state power) may not tread.

The right of religious freedom—which includes, as the Council taught, the claim that "no one is to be restrained from acting in accordance with his own beliefs, whether privately *or publicly*, whether alone *or in association with others*, within due limits"[24]—is also helpful in establishing that distinction between society and the state which is fundamental to the liberal democratic project. Democracy, in theory and in practice, rests upon the understandings that society is prior to the state, and that the state exists to serve society, not the other way around. Social institutions[25] have a logical, historical, and one might even say ontological priority over institutions of government. Among the many social institutions that have persistently claimed this distinctive priority are religious institutions and, in the Gelasian tradition, the Christian Church.

Thus the public dimension of the right of religious freedom is a crucial barrier against the totalitarian temptation, in either its Leninist or its mobocracy form. Some things in a democracy— indeed, the very things that are the building-blocks of democracy, i.e., basic human rights—are not up for a vote. Democratic politics are not merely procedural politics; democracies are substantive experiments whose successful working-out requires certain habits (virtues) and attitudes, in addition to the usual democratic procedures. The public meaning of the right of religious freedom reminds us of this, in and out of season. And thus the importance of the right of religious freedom for unbelievers as well as believers, for the secularized American new-class elite as well as for the 90 per cent of the American people who remain stubbornly religious.[26]

In short, and as Murray himself put it at Vatican II and in the *Declaration on Religious Freedom*, Roman Catholicism embraced "the political doctrine of . . . the juridical state . . . [i.e.] government as constitutional and limited in function—its primary function being juridical, namely, the protection and promotion of the rights of man and the facilitation of the performance of man's native duties."[27] The juridical or constitutional state is ruled by consent, not by coercion or by claims of divine right. The state itself stands under the judgment of moral norms that transcend it, moral norms whose constitutional and/or legal expression can be found in bills of rights. Moreover, religious liberty, constitutionally and legally protected, desacralizes politics and thereby opens up the possibility of a politics of consent. Where, in the modern world, could such constitutionally regulated, limited, consensual states be found? The question, posed, seemed to answer itself: in liberal democratic states.

Thus the path to an official Roman Catholic affirmation of democracy had been cleared, and indeed the obligatory ends of a morally worthy democratic *polis* specified, in this American-shaped development of social doctrine on the matter of the fundamental human right of religious freedom.

THE CONTEMPORARY DISCUSSION

Pope John Paul II has deepened and intellectually extended the Catholic human rights revolution during his pontificate, not least by explicitly connecting it to the democratic revolution in world politics.

This extension undoubtedly reflects the pope's personal experience in Poland, where the "parchment barriers" (as Madison would have called them) of Communist constitutions and other forms of political flim-flam have illustrated precisely how important it is that rights be secured by the structure of governmental institutions, as well as by the habits and attitudes of a people. Here, again, we see how the totalitarian project in the twentieth century has been, paradoxically, a prod to the extension and evolution of Catholic social teaching.

Challenging Liberation Theology

John Paul II has also had to contend with the phenomenon of the various theologies of liberation. While liberation theology is a reality vastly more complex (and, just possibly, of considerably less long-term importance) than what has typically been presented in the U.S. secular media, the sundry theologies of liberation share a pronounced skepticism, at times verging on hostility, to what they often term the bourgeois formalism of liberal democracy. Whether liberation theology represents a genuinely distinctive phenomenon in Catholic history, or rather the old Iberian fondness for altar-and-throne arrangements in a unitary state moved from right to left on the political spectrum, is an intriguing question, the full exploration of which is beyond the scope of this essay. What is clear is that, by the early 1980s, the theologies of liberation had evolved, in this matter of Catholicism and democracy, along a rather different path than that taken by the Roman magisterium.

Closing the widening breach between official Catholic social teaching and the theologies of liberation, and challenging the currents in the latter that were most out of phase with the developments sketched above, was the task undertaken by the Congregation for the Doctrine of the Faith in its two Instructions on liberation theology, the first published in 1984 and the second in 1986.

The 1984 "Instruction on Certain Aspects of the 'Theology of Liberation,' " issued by the Congregation with the pope's personal authority, acknowledged that liberation was an important theme in Christian theology. It frankly faced the overwhelming facts of poverty and degradation in much of Latin America, and argued that the Church indeed has a special love for, and responsibility to, the poor.

On the other hand, the Instruction rejected a number of themes that had been key teachings of the various theologies of liberation. Among these the Instruction cited: the primary locating of sin in social, economic, and political structures; the class-struggle model of society and history and related analyses of structural violence; the subordination of the individual to the collectivity; the transformation of the concepts of good and evil into strictly political categories, and the subsequent loss of a sense of transcendent dimension to the moral life; the concept of a partisan Church; and an "exclusively political interpretation" of the death of Christ.[28]

But for our purposes here, the most crucial passage in the 1984 Instruction was the following:

One needs to be on guard against the politicization of existence, which, misunderstanding the entire meaning of the Kingdom of God and the transcendence of the person, begins to sacralize politics and betray the religion of the people in favor of the projects of the revolution.[29]

Against the core dynamic of the Catholic human rights revolution, the theologies of liberation were proposing a return to the altar-and-throne arrangements of the past—this time buttressed by the allegedly scientific accomplishments of Marxist social analysis. With this new monism came, inevitably, the use of coercive state power against individuals and against the Church. The politics of consent were again being threatened by the politics of coercion. In short, the theologies of liberation had broken with the modern retrieval of the Gelasian tradition as it had evolved in the teaching of the Second Vatican Council and the social teaching of John Paul II.

The 1986 "Instruction on Christian Freedom and Liberation" pushed the official Roman discussion even further toward an open endorsement of the moral superiority of democratic politics in this passage:

> There can only be authentic development in a social and political system which respects freedoms and fosters them through the participation of everyone. This participation can take different forms; it is necessary in order to guarantee a proper pluralism in institutions and in social initiatives. It ensures, notably by a real separation between the powers of the State, the exercise of human rights, also protecting them against possible abuses on the part of the public powers. No one can be excluded from this participation in social and political life for reasons of sex, race, color, social condition, language, or religion. . . .
>
> When the political authorities regulate the exercise of freedoms, they cannot use the pretext of the demands of public order and security in order to curtail those freedoms systematically. Nor can the alleged principle of national security, or a narrowly economic outlook, or a totalitarian conception of social life, prevail over the value of freedom and its rights.[30]

"Sollicitudo": Support for Democracy-Building

The politicization of the Gospel—its reduction to a partisan, mundane program—and the re-sacralization of politics were decisively rejected by the 1984 Instruction. The 1986 Instruction taught that participatory politics were morally superior to the politics of vanguards, whether aristocratic or Marxist-Leninist. The linkage between these themes and the positive task of democracy-building was made in late 1987 by the encyclical *Sollicitudo Rei Socialis*.

Sollicitudo's portrait of the grim situation of Third World countries was based on an analysis more complex than that in the encyclical it was written to commemorate, Paul VI's *Populorum Progressio* (1967). Where Paul tended to locate primary (some would say, virtually exclusive) responsibility for underdevelopment in the developed world, John Paul II argued that responsibility for the world's underclass was not unilinear, and involved "undoubtedly grave instances of omissions on the part of the developing countries themselves, and especially on the part of those holding economic and political power."[31] In a more positive vein (and here extending the Catholic human rights revolution in explicitly structural/political terms), John Paul II taught that economic development would be impossible without the evolution of what would be called, in Western terms, the civil society: in the pope's own words, "the developing nations themselves should favor the self-affirmation of each citizen, through access to a wider culture and a free flow of information."[32]

Yet the enhanced moral and cultural skills of a people were not enough, the pope continued. Important as they were, they would not yield "integral human development" if the peoples in question remained the vassals or victims of inept, hidebound, ideologically rigid, and/or kleptocratic dictatorships. Thus, true development required that Third World countries "reform certain unjust structures, and in particular their political institutions, in order to replace corrupt, dictatorial, and authoritarian forms of government by democratic and participatory ones."[33]

In short, in *Sollicitudo Rei Socialis*, the formal leadership of the Roman Catholic Church confirmed its support for the democratic revolution in world politics. As John Paul II said of this striking phenomenon of the 1980s,

> This is a process which we hope will spread and grow stronger. For the health of a political community—as expressed in the free and responsible participation of all citizens in public affairs, in the rule of law, and in respect for and promotion of human

rights—is the necessary condition and sure guarantee of the development of the whole individual and of all people.[34]

Sollicitudo in fact brought Catholic social theory into congruence with Catholic social practice during the pontificate of John Paul II. Whether the locale has been El Salvador, Chile, Nicaragua, Paraguay, Poland, the Philippines, South Korea, or sub-Saharan Africa, John Paul II has spoken in consistent support (and, in Poland, rather more than that) of the replacement of "corrupt, dictatorial, and authoritarian forms of government" by "democratic and participatory ones." And as for criticism that his preaching on behalf of human rights and democracy constituted an unbecoming interference in politics, the pope had this to say to a reporter who asked him about such carping, while pope and press were en route to Chile and Paraguay in 1987: "Yes, yes, I am not the evangelizer of democracy, I am the evangelizer of the Gospel. To the Gospel message, of course, belong all the problems of human rights, and if democracy means human rights it also belongs to the message of the Church."[35] From religious conversion, to moral norms, to institutions and patterns of governance, the pope's sense of priorities is clear; but so too is the connection between Catholic social teaching and the democratic revolution.

Deepening Democratic Culture

None of this should be taken to suggest, of course, that the Church of the 1990s and beyond will be an uncritical or naïve celebrant of the democratic possibility. As John Paul II made clear during his pastoral visit to the United States in 1987, democratic polities must always remind themselves of the transcendent norms of judgment to which they hold themselves open. Most particularly, today, this means deepening the democracies' understanding of human freedom. As the pope put it in 1987, speaking of the United States,

Among the many admirable values of this country there is one that stands out in particular. It is freedom. The concept of freedom is part of the very fabric of this nation as a political community of free people. Freedom is a great gift, a blessing of God.

From the beginning of America, freedom was directed to forming a well-ordered society and to promoting its peaceful life. Freedom was channeled to the fullness of human life, to the preservation of human dignity, and to the safeguarding of human rights. An experience of ordered freedom is truly part of the history of this land.

This is the freedom that America is called upon to live and guard and transmit. She is called to exercise it in such a way that it will also benefit the cause of freedom in other nations and among other peoples.[36]

Thus did the Bishop of Rome endorse the moral intention of the American experiment in the categories of the Catholic Whig tradition, as exemplified by Acton and his postulate that freedom is a matter, not of doing what you want, but of having the right to do what you ought.

Cardinal Joseph Ratzinger, chief intellectual architect of the two Instructions on Christian freedom and liberation, has been another challenging critic of the gap between intention and performance in the established democracies. Ratzinger, like John Courtney Murray, is particularly concerned that democracy not be reduced to what the American Jesuit would have called "an ensemble of procedures" with no substantive foundation. As the cardinal put it in a 1979 essay,

Democracy is by its nature linked to *eunomia*, to the validity of good law, and can only remain democracy in such a relationship. Democracy in this way is never the mere domination of majorities, and the mechanism whereby majorities are provided must be guided by the common rule of *nomos*, of what internally is law, that is, under the rule of values that form a binding presupposition for the majority too. . . .

. . . Democracy is only capable of functioning when conscience is functioning, and . . . this latter has nothing to say if it is not guided and influenced by the fundamental moral values of Christianity, values which are capable of realization even in the absence of any specific acknowledgment of Christianity and indeed in the context of non-Christian religion.[37]

These developments in Catholic social teaching and the Church's theology have had significant effects "on the ground," as papal teaching and Catholic reformist practice have, in a variety of locales, become a powerful support for the democratic revolution—and a means for keeping that revolution from spilling over into anarchy. Catholic lay organizations, supported by their local bishops and by the Holy See, have proven an indispensable part of the democratic transitions in Spain and Portugal. The Church is clearly aligned on the side of democracy in Latin America, to the discomfort of *caudillos* right and left. In Poland, Czechoslovakia, and Lithuania, the Church has been at the forefront of the democratic churnings in the world's last empire. In East Asia, the Church was the chief domestic institutional support for the democratic insurgency that toppled Ferdinand Marcos and installed Corazon Aquino, and church leaders and laity played important roles in the transition to democracy in South Korea. This complex pattern of activism was buttressed by, even as it influenced, the Church's moral case for the democratic alternative—a case that combined idealism and realism in an impressively sophisticated mix.

Thus Sir Michael Howard's identification of the "other twentieth-century revolution" seems, at the start of the 1990s, not quite so surprising after all, and in fact remarkably prescient.

ISSUES FOR THE FUTURE

The dialectic between the evolution of Catholic social teaching and the democratic revolution can be expected to continue. Among the issues that may rise to the front of the intellectual agenda are the following.

1. Catholic social teaching, in the United States and in Rome, should more fully integrate the experience of the American Founding—including the Founders' and Framers' philosophical justification for their revolutionary activity—into its reflection on the quest for human freedom. There remains a tendency in Rome to view the modern history of that quest through primarily Continental filters. Thus the seminal 1986 "Instruction on Christian Freedom and Liberation" could argue that "it was above all . . . at the French Revolution that the call to freedom rang out with full force. Since that time, many have regarded future history as an irresistible process of liberation inevitably leading to an age in which man, totally free at last, will enjoy happiness on this earth."[38]

But there was another revolutionary tradition in the late eighteenth century. Contrary to the revolution of 1789, the American revolution of 1776 and 1787 was a deliberate extension rather than repudiation of the central political tradition of the West. Beginning with its declaration of inalienable rights given by "Nature, and Nature's God," the American Revolution was channeled into the process of constitution-making, not into the sanguinary excesses of Jacobinism.

The current historiography of the American Founding stresses that the Founders and Framers, far from being the radical Lockean individualists and libertarian Smithite merchants portrayed by Vernon Louis Parrington and Charles Beard, were in fact thoroughly convinced that the success of the American experiment required a citizenry that would live the life of "public virtue, public liberty, [the] public happiness of republicanism, the humane sociability of the Scottish Enlightenment." For the American Founders and Framers, in other words, "the concept of public virtue stood at or near the center of 'republicanism.' " They were moral realists, not antinomians; knowing that all men were sinners, they tried to devise "republican institutions which could preserve liberty in virtue's absence."[39]

This moral realism of the Founders and Framers is, of course, not identical with the Catholic social ethical tradition of moderate realism as developed by Augustine and Aquinas.[40] There would seem to be, however, important points of connection between the two—a point emphasized by such giants of the American Church as John Carroll, John England, James Gibbons, John Ireland, and John Courtney Murray. An intense conversation with the leadership of the universal Church, as it continues to reflect on the political/institutional implications of the Catholic human rights revolution, needs to take place, and ought to focus at least some of its attention on the dialectic between the American experience of democratic republicanism and the public philosophy undergirding (or failing to undergird) the experiment launched in 1776 and 1787.

If that point is not particularly well understood in Rome today, the problem may lie, not primarily with Rome, but with the successors of Carroll and Gibbons in the American episcopate, and the successors of Murray among American Catholic intellectuals. In both quarters, today, one finds a disturbing phenomenon: men and women who insist on being *American* Catholics but who deep down are profoundly skeptical about, indeed in some cases overtly hostile to, the American experiment.[41] In short, the current episcopal and intellectual leadership of the Church in the United States has not completed the task begun by Gibbons in his 1887 sermon at Santa Maria in Trastevere. It is time to take that task up again— for the sake of the moral deepening of the American experiment, and for the sake of the evolution of Catholic social teaching.

2. *The argument with the various theologies of liberation must continue.* The Vatican Instructions of 1984 and 1986—and the democratic revolution itself in Latin America—have had a beneficial impact on this front. In an interview with the *New York Times* in the summer of 1988, for example, Father Gustavo Gutiérrez of Peru, widely recognized as the father of liberation theology, distanced himself from those of his brethren who deprecate the accomplishments of Latin America's nascent democracies as but bourgeois formalism. "Experience with dictatorship," Father Gutiérrez said, "has made liberation theologians more appreciative of political rights." So, too, have the "changes in Marxist and socialist thinking" in Eastern Europe.[42] So, too, one suspects, have the Vatican Instructions of 1984 and 1986, and the social teaching of John Paul II, in his encyclicals and during his pastoral visits to Latin America.

In short, it is now possible to imagine a second-phase or third-phase liberation theology that supports, rather than deprecates, the democratic revolution and the possibilities it holds out for empowerment of the poor. But to imagine such a development and to find it are, of course, two different things. Today, a liberation theology of democracy is a possibility, not a reality.[43] And so a continued conversation, which is sure to be brisk, remains in order.

3. *Catholic social teaching must also address the problems of religious liberty—and thus of the right-ordering of political communities—that are showing up more frequently in the Church's interface with other world religions.* Militant Hindus in Nepal and India as well as Islamic fundamentalists throughout Africa and Asia are now impeding,

with various degrees of persecutorial vigor, the evangelical and sacramental mission of the Church.

These confrontations raise intriguing new questions for the Catholic human rights revolution and the Church's support for democratic transitions. In many Asian and African locales, or even in a quasi-Western nation such as Haiti, the cultural roots of democracy seem scanty at best. The Church, like democrats throughout the world, has to explore a number of questions here:

What are the cultural prerequisites for successful transitions to democracy? Can these cultural building-blocks of the politics of participation and consent be enhanced or strengthened by the intervention (the term is used neutrally) of external religious forces?

Islam and Hinduism are complex bodies of religious thought. What currents within them are supportive of democratic politics? What currents are opposed? What is the correlation of forces (to borrow from the Marxists) between supporters and opponents?

Catholicism is now formally committed to a strategy of inculturation in its missionary work.[44] What is the relation, if any, between the inculturation of the Gospel and the inculturation of human rights norms and political institutions generally perceived in Third World arenas to be Western—and thus suspect? How, in other words, does the Church concretely give expression to John Paul II's comment cited earlier, that "to the Gospel message . . . belong all the problems of human rights, and if democracy means human rights it also belongs to the message of the Church"—and do so without appearing to be the agent of Western cultural imperialism?

In sum, then, the new official Roman Catholic support for the democratic revolution in world politics raises at least as many question as it answers, for both theology and political theory, both evangelization and political action. The "other revolution" will, it seems, be an ongoing one.

PART TWO

Peace and the Economy, Again

3

The *Tranquillitas Ordinis* Debate: A Memoir With Prescriptions

Two years into the "kinder, gentler" Bush era, with the ideological fires banked across the broad center of American reliopolitical opinion, it may be difficult for some to remember the animosity, indeed loathing, that Ronald Reagan and his administration aroused in the minds, hearts, and adrenal glands of some American Catholic religious leaders, and many American Catholic intellectuals, throughout the 1980s. If the Bush presidency affords religious thinkers and activists as blurred a target as it does op-ed commentators, such was surely not the case during the preceding eight years. Then, the inheritors of the enthusiasms of the sixties knew the enemy and saw him clearly, red in tooth and claw: Ronald Reagan, and all his works, and all his empty promises.

This was especially true in foreign policy, as exemplified by the Catholic activist-led agitations against the administration's nuclear strategy and Central American policy. Reagan's determination to clarify the stakes in the Cold War, and his administration's commitment to reversing the pattern of Western retreat that had defined the geopolitics of the 1970s, were a direct challenge to the convictions and interests of religious activists, fresh from their paradigmatic triumph in Nicaragua in 1979–80. And they were no less offensive to American liberal and radical religious intellectuals who had spent the previous decade imbibing the themes (and, perhaps more significantly, the sensibility) of Habermasian neo-Marxism (itself, a "kinder, gentler" variant of the Real Thing) and the sundry

Latin American theologies of liberation. In these worlds, where "history" was "on the side of" the international Left, Reagan, and such emblematic members of his administration as Jeane J. Kirkpatrick and Elliott Abrams, could not but appear as so many dangerous, simian throwbacks. The polemics followed accordingly.

Strirring Up the Animals

In this febrile climate I published *Tranquillitas Ordinis: The Present Failure and Future Promise of American Catholic Thought on War and Peace*.[1] And a most instructive row ensued. The reviewer in the Sunday *New York Times Book Review*, perhaps predictably, dismissed my argument as having no more credibility than a child's fairy tale.[2] Not so predictably, the reviewer in the radical *Catholic Worker* welcomed *Tranquillitas Ordinis* as "a lively, major work which is a significant contribution to the Catholic debate on war and peace."[3] *Commonweal* devoted large portions of two issues to explaining the error of my ways.[4] And *Tranquillitas Ordinis* became the first book in decades to merit essay-length disapprobation in the most prestigious journal in American Catholic theology, *Theological Studies*.[5] On the other, other hand, Father Avery Dulles, S.J., a frequent *Theological Studies* contributor generally regarded as the plumbline of moderation and good sense among Catholic theologians in the United States, saw *Tranquillitas Ordinis* as "an imposing contribution to the current debate about peace and weaponry. . . . Thoroughly researched, cogently reasoned, lucidly organized, and temperately expressed, this book may change the state of the question."[6]

It probably didn't do *that*, but *Tranquillitas Ordinis* certainly did, as Mencken would have said, stir up the animals.

Which was, I confess, at least part of its intention. David Hollenbach, the reviewer in *Theological Studies* (and a man with whom I remain on friendly personal terms), got this much right, at least: *Tranquillitas Ordinis* was quite frankly "designed to change the state of the question in church discussions of the theology, ethics, and politics of peace and war in our day."[7] I don't remember having that as my explicit goal when I came to the Woodrow Wilson International Center for Scholars in September 1984 to spend a year thinking and writing about the current state of the Catholic debate over America's role in world politics. But at some point, during the next six months of reading and pondering the relevant literature (the periodical portion of which alone filled a four-drawer file cabinet), I became convinced that things were in far worse shape than I had imagined: worse, not simply because the foreign-policy commentaries and prescriptions of the Church's intellectual and religious leaders seemed so extravagantly wrong-headed, but because they represented, in varying degrees, a break with classic Catholic understandings about the ethics and politics of international public life. In some instances, among the radicals, that break was self-conscious and deliberate; in most cases, though, it was unconscious—precisely because the mainstream of the American Catholic establishment had convinced itself, between 1965 and 1980 (and under the influence of the radicals), that it had precious little heritage of thought on war and peace, either to develop or to abandon.

Batting One for Three

Three things were needed, it seemed to me in early 1985. First, I had to demonstrate that there was in fact a "Catholic heritage" of serious moral and political reflection on these matters, and an explicitly *American* Catholic heritage to boot. Then I would have to show that this heritage had been ignored or dismissed, even to the point of abandonment. And, finally, I should try to demonstrate how the classic heritage, even with its faults and *lacunae* (which I spent half a chapter outlining), was still a solid foundation on which a contemporary theology and politics of peace and freedom might be built. The entire enterprise, I also decided, should be prefaced by a more literary meditation, reflecting on the dilemma of a humanity caught, in a distinctively modern way, between the fire of war and the pit of totalitarianism.

Three years after publication, it seems to me that the first third of the book—my attempt to define with some creativity the "Catholic heritage" on matters of war and peace, and especially the American contribution to that heritage—has been more or less ignored. Some attention has been paid to my sketch of the thought of Father John Courtney Murray, S.J., whom I consider the paradigm of a Catholic intellectual engaged responsibly and vigorously in the public debate over U.S. foreign policy. One or two commentators have noted, approvingly, my claim that the Augustinian/Thomistic just-war tradition carries within itself a *ius ad pacem*, a concept of peace as rightly ordered and dynamic political community, that gives deeper meaning to the classic *ius ad bellum* and *ius in bello* (the moral criteria for assessing the justice of a given war, and the morality of military action within it). But my suggestion that the American experience of Catholicism had pointed the Church toward a new understanding of democracy as the modern realization of Augustine's classic definition of peace as *tranquillitas ordinis*, the "tranquillity of order," seems not to have provoked the kind of debate for which I had hoped.

Nor did my prescriptions for a revivified Catholic theology and politics of peace-through-freedom do much to set the boundaries for the next phase of the argument. Critics from the left were wont to dismiss my proposals as a (perhaps) more benign form of Reaganism; how "Reaganism," however parsed, squared with my calls for a new pacifist/just-war dialogue and a new attentiveness to the possibilities of non-violent resistance to tyranny, was never made altogether clear by the brethren *à gauche*. And even friendlier reviewers missed what turned out, in happy retrospect, to be the most prescient of the book's suggestions, viz., that a strategy of "pluralization" leading to democratization should guide U.S. policy toward the Communist world.[8]

What *did* get the critical and polemical juices flowing was the book's second section: my analysis of what I termed the "abandonment of the heritage" by Catholic intellectuals and activists from, roughly, 1965 through 1980, and my claim that this "abandonment" had decisively influenced the U.S. Catholic bishops' 1983 pastoral letter, *The Challenge of Peace*, and their positions on U.S. policy in Central America throughout the 1980s. In short, the polemics surrounding *Tranquillitas Ordinis*—polemics that, I believe, obscured the book's first and third sections and precluded the debate that might have been engaged on the issues I raised there—had to do with my reading of the immediate past, and its impact on the American Catholic present.

Why that happened, and the terms in which it happened, are matters of more than personal interest, for they crystallize and distill, in a particularly sharp way and on both sides of the Great Reagan Divide, many of the key themes in religious thought about foreign policy in the 1980s. For that reason, it may be useful to look back briefly at the "*Tranquillitas Ordinis* debate" to see what lessons might be learned for the future of the argument over religiously grounded moral reasoning and U.S. foreign policy.

GIVING OFFENSE

Most observers would take it as the quintessence of the obvious to suggest that American Catholicism's intellectual and religious leaders moved to the left, in their thinking about U.S. foreign policy, in the period between the close of the Second Vatican Council (1965) and the inauguration of Ronald Reagan in 1981.[9] Yet defining the obvious, and, perhaps more to the point, suggesting that this turn to the left involved discontinuities with some of the key themes that had animated classic Catholic social and political thinking since the days of Augustine and Aquinas, quickly got me labeled a "polemicist" by people who didn't visibly blanch when the archbishop of Seattle described the Trident submarine facility in his diocese as "the Auschwitz of Puget Sound."[10] Why?

In part, to go back to the beginning, because of the *odium religiosum* that was visited upon the Reagan administration in general, and President Reagan in particular, by the liberal American Catholic establishment in the early 1980s. Sharp criticism, bordering on moral dismissal, of Reagan and his henchpersons as boobs at best and malign warmongers at worst was a kind of admission ticket to the "mainstream" Catholic debate in the 1980s. I declined to indulge in ritual Reagan-bashing, and I was thus a suspect. Those suspicions hardened when I also declined to accept two myths that had deeply penetrated the Church's intellectual and religious leadership: that Jonathan Schell's nuclear apocalypticism provided an appropriate moral and political starting point for the debate on nuclear weapons and strategy, and that the Nicaraguan Sandinistas and the Salvadoran FMLN guerrillas were on the side of the angels (and "the side of history") in Central America.

The debate on Central America lasted longer, and may yet have a deeper impact on the future of the Catholic bishops' address to the pursuit of peace in the modern world. But it was the nuclear argument—preceding and surrounding the composition of *The Challenge of Peace*—that put the "reception" of the classic Catholic heritage to its sharpest test, and thus best illustrated how that heritage had been, to put it bluntly but accurately, abandoned.

The Nuclear Issue

How fevered had the discussion of the nuclear issue in Catholic circles become in the early 1980s? Highly fevered, indeed. The second draft of *The Challenge of Peace*, for example, contained this startling assertion: "The destructive potential of the nuclear powers threatens the sovereignty of God over the world he has brought into being. We could destroy his work."[11] As I wrote at the time, perhaps more flippantly than the circumstances warranted, it might come as news to God that his sovereignty over creation was threatened by human idiocies. Mercifully, this particular Schellism didn't make it into the final draft of the bishops' letter. But that it appeared in any draft at all suggests that the American Catholic debate had broken loose from its theological moorings in the early 1980s, under the impact of certain themes from the secular political culture that had a surface resemblance to Christian apocalyptic but in fact carried a very different, survivalist message.

Paralleling this collapse of apocalyptic into survivalism was a foreshortening of the American Catholic establishment's eschatological horizon: the arrival of the Kingdom that Christians believe will come "in the fullness of time" could, in fact, be accelerated by political activism in the here-and-now. Or so it was taught by numerous Catholic activists and not a few Catholic intellectuals. Forms of political utopianism, in other words, began to color the Catholic debate on foreign policy. Conflict, which generations of Catholic scholars had understood as a constant of the human condition (the political meaning, if you will, of the doctrine of original sin), was now to be regarded as epiphenomenal: a matter of bad communication, or misunderstanding, or jingoism. The Reagan administration's insistence that the world was a dangerous place, and the president's (initial) fondness for framing the Great Issue in world politics in explicitly ideological and moral terms (the decent West vs. the "evil empire"), were thus like fingernails raked down a blackboard to American Catholic activists raised on a fairly steady diet of anti–anti-Communism and neo-isolationism since the Vietnam period, and convinced that the creation of "a world that is human" (as one chief activist center put it) was essentially a matter of will. Those who lacked the will were, *ipso facto*, evil. Or, at the very least, morally suspect.

Compounding this utopian muddleheadedness in the activist community was an insistence, by several prominent intellectuals in the small guild of Catholic experts on ethics and international affairs, on the utter distinctiveness of the world situation in the 1980s. Thus David Hollenbach, in his *Theological Studies* review of *Tranquillitas Ordinis*, would chastise me on the grounds that I "effectively ignored the several qualitative transformations of the war-and-peace problematic brought about by every new generation of nuclear strategy and weaponry since 1945."[12] The statement still puzzles me. What did Hollenbach mean by "several *qualitative* transformations," particularly if "the war-and-peace problematic" was understood to be, in the first instance, the moral argument as framed by just-war theory? Nothing essential had changed here. No doubt the arms-control side of things had gotten considerably more complex with the advent of MIRVing, cruise missiles, and the like. But these technological developments hadn't changed the basic structure of the moral argument.

What *had* changed, of course, was the tone quality of the United States government in its discussion of nuclear weapons. The Reagan administration's commitment to modernization of the American nuclear deterrent, set in the context of its vigorous anti-Communism and its boisterously old-fashioned American patriotism, deeply shook the American Catholic intellectual elite—as it did the "cultured despisers" of Reaganite conservatism throughout the American academy. And by "shook" I mean to convey something of the visceral loathing for, and fear of, Reagan administration nuclear policy that was pandemic in these worlds. Most Americans knew in their bones that Ronald Reagan had no desire to fight a nuclear war. But the American Catholic intellectual establishment was much less certain of that. And its perceptions of reality—and of *Tranquillitas Ordinis*—were skewed accordingly.

Linking Peace and Freedom

The book would also give offense by its unapologetic anti-Communism, its disdain for the regime in the Soviet Union, and its defense of liberal democracy as the modern form of governance most reflective of the classic Catholic definition of peace as *tranquillitas ordinis*, dynamic and rightly ordered political community. The nuclear fear shaped this axis of deprecation, of course. Thus David Hollenbach charged that I had not thought through the implications of my call for linkage between arms reduction and political change in the USSR, and worried "what the costs of such linkage might be."[13]

My view is that I *had* thought these things through, and had come to a conclusion that Hollenbach evidently found disturbing: in the crunch, the United States should stand firm for human rights and for democratization in the USSR, even at the short-term cost of this or that arms "control" agreement. Holding the Soviet Union accountable to international human rights standards to which it has freely adhered does not create obstacles to arms reduction. If Soviet leaders perceive such reductions to be in their national interest, then they will proceed.[14] The successful conclusion of the INF treaty gives empirical weight to this theoretical point.[15]

The situation will be far more complex in the 1990s, when "linkage" has to do not so much with individual prisoners of conscience as with the rights of self-determination of peoples within the Soviet internal empire (such as the people of the Baltic republics and Ukraine). But the basic point I was making remains, I believe, valid: for so long as the Soviet Union remains the abnormal state/empire it is, for just so long will it remain a dangerous adversary with whom radical arms reduction leading to real disarmament will be unlikely.

Betting on Democracy

Viewed through one prism, the entire argument of *Tranquillitas Ordinis* came down to this: that American Catholicism had forgotten, and needed to recover, what was most distinctive about its own appropriation and extension of the classic Catholic heritage of thought on war and peace—the notion that peace, in the modern world, would come through institutions of freedom, within and among nations. Democracy, in other words, was the best available expression, under modern conditions (i.e., mass populations; religious, cultural, and/or ethnic pluralism; rapid social and economic mobility; the communications revolution), of the classic Catholic concept of peace as *tranquillitas ordinis*.

Those for whom nuclear weapons were the overriding moral issue in contemporary international public life were uncomfortable with this claim. If it were taken seriously, might arms control be held hostage to some chimerical quest for political transformation in the Soviet Union and the Warsaw Pact? Equally disturbed were those for whom the Sandinista revolution in Nicaragua (and the hoped-for FMLN revolution in El Salvador), rather than the American Revolution of 1776 and 1787, provided the best moral paradigm for the incarnation of *tranquillitas ordinis*.

The remarkable events of 1989 and 1990 in east central Europe, the Soviet Union, and Latin America have made the point about democracy far more eloquently than I possibly could in *Tranquillitas Ordinis*. That the Warsaw Pact is a thing of the past, and that peace seems to be breaking out over most of east central Europe, has little or nothing to do with relative numbers of nuclear weapons, tanks, tactical aircraft, or ground forces, and everything to do with the transformation of the regimes in Poland, Hungary, Czechoslovakia, Bulgaria, Romania, and East Germany.

Similarly, in Central America, the Nicaraguan people's decisive rejection of the Sandinista government and the continuing failure of the Salvadoran FMLN to instigate a "popular uprising" testify to the crucial importance of the nature of regimes in determining the prospects for peace in a troubled region. For fifteen years, American Catholic activists, and not a few Catholic intellectuals, insisted that the problem of peace in Central America was essentially a problem of poverty, which was to be assuaged by vaguely Marxist (and certainly socialist) schemes of redistribution. The people of Central America remain desperately and unnecessarily poor. But the chances for peace, and for the economic development that can come with peace, have improved significantly because of the defeat of the Sandinistas and the transition to democratic regimes throughout the region.

In his *Theological Studies* review essay, David Hollenbach accused me of promoting "a kind of crusade for democracy" as the sovereign remedy for the world's multiple ills.[16] Happily, and through his reflection on the events of the late 1980s, Hollenbach has now come around to the view that *The Challenge of Peace* would indeed have been strengthened had it paid rather more attention to the peace-and-freedom linkage and to the possibility that political transformation (i.e., adherence to human rights standards and a gradual process of democratization) in the Communist world could significantly lessen the danger of nuclear war. In a 1989 lecture at Catholic University, for example, Hollenbach argued that "there is a sense in which the 1983 pastoral letter is already dated." While he still disagreed with my "overall assessment" of the letter, he said, he was "willing to concede" that, had the bishops given the "political and ideological questions" of the Cold War "greater prominence from the beginning" of their argument, their letter would have been less subject to the kind of criticism I and others had mounted.[17]

MORE BONES OF CONTENTION

Three other controversies that emerged in the post–*Tranquillitas Ordinis* to-and-fro might be mentioned briefly.

"Abandonment of the Heritage"

There was considerable, and perhaps in some cases justified, consternation over my use of "abandonment" to characterize the position of the American Catholic intellectual and religious leadership vis-à-vis its classic moral heritage of reflection on issues of peace, freedom, and security. David Hollenbach, for example, wrote that "the charge of the abandonment of the tradition is theologically and psychologically . . . provocative" in the Roman Catholic context, given the nature of the Church's magisterium and the commitment of its current leadership to stand in a line of continuity with the Church's moral teaching.[18] Since my purposes in using the phrase "the heritage abandoned" have been controverted, and from my point of view somewhat misunderstood, a bit of clarification is in order.

I used the term "the heritage" deliberately, for I did not mean to imply that what had been "abandoned" was "the tradition" as that term is understood in its gravest sense: the deposit of Catholic faith that is found in the Scriptures, the Fathers of the Church, and the first seven ecumenical councils. That deposit of faith, which will define Christian orthodoxy until the Kingdom comes, has to do with the central affirmations of the creed: revelation and grace, the incarnation and resurrection, the Trinity, the Church as the chosen (if earthen) vessel for the continuation of Christ's saving work. These affirmations are boundary-setters in an irreducible way; they are *status confessionis* beliefs.

The core tenets of Catholic social ethics—personalism, the common good, subsidiarity, "solidarity"—are not of such dogmatic or theological density. But they do constitute a consistent (and persistent) attempt to relate the chief dogmatic affirmations of the creed to the Church's approach to the fundamental questions of life in society. One challenges the normative status of these tenets, perhaps not at the peril of one's soul, but certainly at the peril of one's religious-intellectual integrity.

Finally, there is another level of Catholic understanding, the level that I referred to as "the heritage." Here we are talking about more contingent judgments—about principles and institutions for the right-ordering of a just society, about interpretations of the lessons of history, about the prudential application of principle to complex realities. But to call these judgments more contingent is not to deny them an important measure of *gravitas*. They have behind them, not the weight of dogmatic definition, but the weight of sophisticated reflection tempered by hard experience.

When Catholic intellectuals and bishops, during the period 1965–85, failed to develop (and in some cases ridiculed) the just-war tradition; when they indulged in a kind of sentimental pacifism drawn from Pelagian or semi-Pelagian understandings of the human condition; when they denied or radically minimized the threat to human decency posed by Marxism-Leninism, or when they dismissed those who challenged such a denial as McCarthyite; when concern over military hardware drove their understanding of peace, rather than their concept of peace framing their approach to weapons issues—when all these things happened (and only the willfully ignorant or the ideologically obsessed now deny that they did), there was, I submit, an "abandonment of the heritage." There was not heresy, although some of the Pelagian currents in the debate bumped up against the boundaries of orthodoxy. There may not have been conscious rejection. But there was abandonment.

I believe a fair-minded reading of *Tranquillitas Ordinis* will not sustain the claim that I accused the bishops of being crypto-heretics who willfully discarded key elements of Catholic dogma. I do believe, however, that the Catholic social ethical heritage of moral reasoning on matters of war and peace, as it had been developed in the American Church for many generations, was indeed abandoned, in the main, by those who drove the American Catholic debate on these issues in the period between the Council and *The Challenge of Peace*. One can affirm the Nicene Creed, accept the key tenets of modern Catholic social thought, work within a form of the just-war tradition—and still be involved in an "abandonment of the heritage."

In his review of *Tranquillitas Ordinis*, Avery Dulles asked whether I hadn't overstressed the elements of discontinuity I discerned in *The Challenge of Peace*. After all, Father Dulles wrote, in their letter the bishops "accept the standard just war criteria; they reject unilateral disarmament; they disavow pacifism as an option for the state; they conditionally approve of the strategy of deterrence; they appear to favor gradual, mutual, and verifiable disarmament; they recognize the grave threats posed by Soviet imperialism, and they celebrate the broad range of freedoms in the United States."[19]

But the issue is not whether these pieces of "the heritage" were present in the letter; they were, and I freely conceded that they were. The issue was, and is, the intellectual and moral *ordering* of the argument, and the excessive weight *The Challenge of Peace* gave to the nuclear-weapons starting point. The issue is, and was, the letter's confusing attempt to straddle the just-war/pacifist debate through the chimera of "nuclear pacifism"—a maneuver that reinforced the pacifists' claim that theirs was, well, the *really* Christian tradition. And, most importantly, the issue was, and is, the utter absence in *The Challenge of Peace* of any developed meditation on "peace" as *tranquillitas ordinis*, as rightly ordered and dynamic political community.

When the people of Krakow and Prague and Leipzig and Berlin and Budapest accomplished the Revolution of 1989, and strengthened peace through the institutions of freedom, American Catholics ought to have known that what was happening in east central Europe was an extraordinary vindication of their Church's classic concept of peace. American Catholics didn't know that, though, because they hadn't been told about that heritage for a very long time.

Finally, on this point, the failure of the intellectual and religious leaders of the Church to challenge the continued vulgarization of *The Challenge of Peace* by religious educators and activists—a process by which the radicals and many pacifists have attempted to achieve hermeneutically what they were unable to accomplish on the floor of the National Conference of Catholic Bishops—has compounded the misemphases and difficulties of the letter itself, and given them a wholly unwarranted new life for the future.[20]

The Politics of Being Pastorally Epistolary

The reception of *Tranquillitas Ordinis* was also shaped by the degree to which various commentators thought the book served, or dis-served, their favored parties in the contemporary internal politics of American Catholicism. Thus the book's criticism of *The Challenge of Peace* was taken in some quarters as an attack on Cardinal Joseph Bernardin of Chicago, who had chaired the bishops' committee charged with drafting the pastoral letter.

It is a sad thing that so much of what passes for debate in the American Church these days is really a matter of intra-ecclesiastical partisan sparring. That I have my differences with Cardinal Bernardin is no secret. But I believe that *TO* treats the cardinal fairly and respectfully—certainly far more fairly and respectfully than some of his defenders treat his critics.

That being said, I think a fair reading of *Tranquillitas Ordinis* would also regard it as a challenge to the generation-long intellectual hegemony, in defining the public face of American Catholicism, of the bishops and staff members of the United States Catholic Conference (USCC) whose work is most directly scrutinized in the book. The "abandonment" image seems to have cut particularly sharply here, for these men had long regarded themselves (and had been so regarded by the liberal Catholic opinion establishment) as the heirs of the great American Catholic social ethical tradition that goes back to Cardinal James Gibbons and his epic 1887 defense of the Knights of Labor. From Gibbons, through the 1919 "Bishops' Program of Social Reconstruction," through the work of Fathers John Cronin and George Higgins in the labor movement, to the exemplary episcopate of Archbishop Paul Hallinan of Atlanta, to the shaping of the National Conference of Catholic Bishops (NCCB) and the USCC by Cardinal John Dearden of Detroit, to *The Challenge of Peace*—according to the standard account, all this was of a piece. I did not see it that way, and I said so. Perhaps more to the point, I showed that there had been discontinuities on eight key focusing issues, and illustrated the impact of this significant ideological shift on *The Challenge of Peace* and the USCC's approach to the tangled problems of Central America.

Tranquillitas Ordinis was published during a time of transition in the American hierarchy, when the cadre of bishops associated with the Hallinan/Dearden/Bernardin view of the Church's role in the public policy arena was beginning to wane in influence, and different forces, concerned with different agendas, were coming to the fore. The book was thus taken, in some quarters, as an attempt to accelerate that process of change.

However, I am in fact far, far less interested in ecclesiastical politicking than in the development of American Catholic social and political thought. I did not criticize the teachings of *The Challenge of Peace* and the USCC's congressional testimony on Central America because I was promoting a different slate of candidates, so to speak. I criticized them because I thought they were mistaken, and I thought they were mistaken because, *inter alia*, they represented a substantive break with "the heritage" as defined above, a heritage that had framed the war-and-peace debate in American Catholicism until the late 1960s.

Taking the Sixties Seriously

The chief thrust of Peter Steinfels's criticism of *Tranquillitas Ordinis* was that I had wildly exaggerated the degree to which New Left teachings drawn from the misnamed "peace movement" of the Vietnam era had shaped subsequent American Catholic reflection on war and peace.

Now, these things are impossible to pin down with algebraic precision, but it seems to me that one clear piece of evidence for my claim can be found precisely in Jay Dolan's review of *Tranquillitas Ordinis* in the *New York Times Book Review*. Here, the director of the country's most prestigious center for the study of American Catholicism, himself a major figure among American Catholic historians, argued that the Catholic Church had had no theory of peace between Augustine and, say, the brothers Berrigan, the just-war tradition having nothing to do with the pursuit of peace. Such an astonishing argument (which I later described on national television, harshly but accurately, as "self-lobotomization") is explicable only, I think, if one takes the sixties very seriously indeed.

During those hyperventilated days, a host of figures taught American Catholics that they were indeed bereft of a theory of peace in their religious and moral tradition. Some argued this with sophistication and tried to do something constructive about it (Thomas Merton, for example). Others indulged in the most extraordinary vulgarization and distortion of Catholic intellectual history in support of their own claims to moral rectitude and political wisdom (Dan Berrigan, for example, in saying that "the kids and I felt that for the first time in a thousand years we were building community around the altar"[21]). But whether the voices in question were serious or frivolous, during the sixties there was a massive deconstruction of the classic Catholic understandings on war-and-peace issues, a deconstruction whose effects remain with us today.

To argue this was not to argue that "the heritage" was without its flaws. I listed them at some length in *Tranquillitas Ordinis*, and speculated that these were precisely the fault lines along which the tremors and quakes of the sixties ran. But in the 1980s, it was very difficult to engage an argument with Catholic partisans of the essential rightness of that decade. Faced with the threat of Reaganism in politics and a Wojtylan "restoration" in the Vatican (and, subsequently, in the NCCB), the Catholic Left, in both its soft and its hard form, hunkered down like a Pedernales jackrabbit in a tornado, as Lyndon Johnson might have said.

Toward the end of the decade there were signs of a new openness to conversation, and I like to think that *Tranquillitas Ordinis* contributed to that. But the initial reception of the book was, clearly, shaped by the ongoing argument over the hermeneutics of the sixties, a period that I seemed to take far more seriously than those of my critics who were far more sympathetic to its teachings.

THE PATH AHEAD

What theological, strategic, and political issues must the American Catholic debate on war and peace, security and freedom, address in the 1990s? If that debate is to make the contribution to the redefinition of American foreign policy of which Catholic social ethical thought is capable, three "reformations" will be required.

1. The Catholic debate must re-politicize *the discussion of "peace" in the American religious community.*

That prescription may come as a shock to those for whom the problem, over the past generation, has been precisely the politicization of Christian witness on matters of war and peace. But what has been called "politicization" would be more accurately termed partisanship or psychologization, depending on whether the prescriber in question has reflected the views of the hard or the soft religious left. The hard left's case for the "defensive" character of Soviet foreign and military policy has moved to the margins of the argument. The soft left's psychologization of international conflict seems destined for a longer run. In the early 1990s it is being applied with particular zeal to the tangled ethnic, religious, and political affairs of the Middle East, where the claim that the roots of conflict are misunderstanding and poor communication can cause a particularly dangerous form of mischief. Here, the flight to psychology from politics can lead, wittingly or unwittingly, to the most awful kinds of politics.

What remains missing from so much of the Catholic (and,

indeed, American religious) debate is the concept of peace as *tranquillitas ordinis*, as "dynamic and rightly ordered political community." That gap might be filled by a reflection on the Revolution of 1989 in east central Europe. It can also be filled by a reflection on the United States itself.

We are, as Ben Wattenberg has argued, the first "universal nation." Pluralism, the basic cultural given of the world in which we now live, was the native condition of our own experiment. The world has always been "plural," of course. But that plurality takes on a distinctive political cast in a world of 747s, microchips, and fiber-optic cables. The world at large has had to learn how to do politics-amidst-pluralism for the past two or three generations. Americans have been doing it—sometimes better, sometimes worse, but doing it—for two centuries.

Thus the American experiment is a microcosm of the world's central dilemma as it presents itself in each day's headlines. Can human beings build political community across the boundaries of race, language, ethnicity, and religion, and amidst the multiple conflicts endemic to pluralism? There are scores of reasons, many of them weighty, for saying, no, it just can't happen. But the American experience and experiment caution against too simplistic a realism.

For the fact remains that, with one terrible break, the United States has formed and sustained political community amidst luxuriant plurality for over two hundred years. We are a multi-racial people. On the street corners of our towns and cities one finds churches of all sorts, a synagogue, and, latterly, a mosque. We are paleoconservatives and neoconservatives, liberals and neoliberals, radicals and agrarian populists. We disagree, often passionately, on anything and everything from abortion to zoo funding. We live in, and hold ourselves accountable to, many communities: family, religious institution, political party, voluntary association. Yet we are, through it all, a *political* community that has settled its arguments about the ordering of our lives, loves, and loyalties without organized mass violence since 1865.

This is no mean accomplishment. One might even say, with due caution and a proper humility before the vagaries of history, that the American experience and experiment have been a miracle in human affairs. Be that as it may, the American experience has also been a vindication of the classic Catholic heritage in its concept of peace as *tranquillitas ordinis*. For that—the "peace of dynamic and rightly ordered political community"—is what has been built here.

The world will remain plural and conflicted. But that stark fact does not necessarily imply the impossibility of political community. The American experiment, the most extensive embodiment in history of the theory of *tranquillitas ordinis*, is a living refutation of the notion that political community requires a numbing uniformity.

"Work for peace," as that term is understood among many religious intellectuals and activists today, rarely takes account of this distinctively Madisonian experience. Were attention to be paid, as Mrs. Loman put it, peace would be "re-politicized" in ways that challenged both the vulgar politicizations and the politico-psycho-babble of the last twenty years or so.

This would not solve all of our problems, to be sure. A reclaiming, through reflection on the American experience and the experience of the Revolution of 1989, of the Augustinian/Thomistic truth that peace in this world is a matter of politics—a matter of political community—ought not to lead us to expect that the rest of the world can, or should, become "like us" in the twinkling of an eye or by a great act of national will. Our century's two great attempts to build world order through political organization, the League of Nations and the United Nations, are sobering in the extreme. The lesson of their failures is that effective political structures for the peaceful resolution of conflict must be built on a base of community. That community did not exist in 1919 or in 1945. Nor at the macrocosmic level does it exist today.

But elements of it do. The world's democracies form a nascent political community, a zone of peace, that now extends westward from the eastern border of Poland to South Korea and down to Australia. Attempts to build international or transnational structures within that zone of peace are immensely difficult, as the experience of NATO and of the European Community has amply demonstrated. But the zone exists. Within it, it is difficult to conceive of a war. That is surely something.

"World order" is thus more than a pious phrase to be invoked over cocktails at the Aspen Institute. It is, in some respects, a reality, and the real question is not *whether* the world is going to be organized but *how*: by what norms, through what structures, with what forms of accountability? The Catholic heritage of *tranquillitas ordinis* can be an immense resource for those thinking through the questions of "ought" that are inevitably engaged in world politics. American Catholics, having had a special experience of *tranquillitas ordinis* in their own lives, ought to be particularly well positioned to contribute to the debate over the building of peace through institutions of freedom in the world.

In the 1990s, then, the "challenge of peace" for American Catholicism will involve deepening our understanding of the connection between peace and freedom; it will also, quite probably, involve expanding the agenda of freedom to include economic freedom. The hard passage from "democratic transition" to "democratic consolidation" in the new democracies of Latin America and east central Europe will require rapid economic growth in those countries, growth that history has shown comes only when a people's entrepreneurial energies are freed from the stifling bonds of commissars or *caudillos*. The experience of countries like Poland and Chile will loom particularly large on the Catholic horizon, and will bear directly on the evolution of Catholic social teaching at the level of the Church's Roman magisterium. American Catholic intellectuals and religious leaders ought to watch these experiments in entrepreneurship with great interest and care.

2. The Catholic debate must help the policy community reformulate and reconsider the question of the use of armed force in response to aggression or aggressive intent.

Assuming, for the sake of the argument, that the Cold War can be brought successfully to an end, the agenda at the intersection of Catholic moral theology and U.S. defense policy will change in a rather dramatic fashion. The nuclear-weapons issue seems likely to fade from its accustomed place at the front of the queue, and there may be a sense, in some quarters, that the really hard questions of an ethically sound defense posture have been more or less resolved.

That assumption would be badly mistaken. Francis Fukuyama notwithstanding, history has not ended, and neither has conflict between and among nations. Indeed, the likely conflict scenarios of the 1990s will put great pressure on the classic just-war theory and its capacity to inform, normatively, the policy debate.

Take, for example, the loathsome combination of crazy states + chemical or gas warheads + ballistic-missile capability: no longer a nightmare, but a harsh reality of international public life. Is there not an entirely new argument here, some will surely ask, in favor of rapidly developing and deploying a strategic-defense capability that will give effective protection against the Libyas and Iraqs of this world? How might that deployment support, rather than further complicate, the continuing effort to pare back superpower nuclear arsenals?

The volatility brought into the world situation by countries like Libya and Iraq, and by subnational terrorist organizations such as the PLO, also raises urgent moral questions about preemptive military action. The classic just-war tradition holds, as one of its criteria *ad bellum*, that the use of armed force must be a "last resort," after other means of resolving a conflict have been tried and have failed. This criterion has come to be understood, in modern Catholic usage, as requiring that a war (or any military action) be defensive in character, i.e., a response to a clear aggression. Without collapsing into the moral crudities of *raison d'état*, can "last resort" be understood in ways that allow for proportionate and discriminate preemptive military action, precisely for the sake of forestalling greater evils? Israel's preemptive 1981 action against Iraq's Osirak nuclear reactor—judged by some Catholic commentators an aggression, but by others a morally appropriate response to what any prudent political leader would have to construe as Iraqi aggressive intent—may well be a paradigm case for the just-war debates of the 1990s.

Peacekeeping through the interposition of military forces will also loom large in the decade to come. Whether the issue is Kashmir (at one level of difficulty) or an imploding Soviet Union (at a far higher magnitude of peril), it seems likely that managing the ethnic and religious strife of the future will require a willingness on the part of states that wish to take responsibility for world order to interpose their own military forces on occasion. Ideally, this would be done under the aegis of an international political authority. But it seems more likely that coalitions of like-minded states will form for this purpose on a case-by-case basis. Criteria for this new form of "intervention" will thus have to be developed.

3. The Church in the United States must make a substantive contribution to what is likely to be the foreign policy debate of the 1990s in the attentive and general publics: the debate between internationalists and isolationists (or, as they would prefer, "nationalists").

Absent this contribution, neither a "re-politicized" Catholic understanding of peace nor a more sophisticated Catholic clarification of the classic just-war principles in light of today's politico-military environment will be of very much use. The waning of the Cold War, and an increased consciousness of the urgent domestic problems facing the American republic in its third century, have combined to make the foreign-policy debate in the early 1990s resemble nothing so much as the arguments of the 1930s. The difference this time, of course, is that the traditional isolationism of the Old Right has been reinforced (and repackaged) by some liberal Democrats who have been deeply influenced by New Left currents of thought, are eager to free up scarce federal dollars for cherished domestic social programs, and are convinced that vigorous campaigning for the "new nationalism" (with its calls for a kind of American economic autarky) will play well with an electorate that has been skeptical about Democratic "toughness" for a generation now.

Meeting the challenge of the old/new isolationism is, at bottom, a matter not so much of economic statistics as of moral argument. For while there are sensible economic and political reasons to defend a prudent internationalism, the most urgent case in favor of an active American engagement with world politics—an engagement aimed at building a larger measure of *tranquillitas ordinis* in international public life—is essentially a case argued on behalf of an "ought." The dean of St. Paul's put it in a form that has not lost its truth for all that it has become a cliché: "No man is an Island, entire of itself." The man who conducts himself as an island diminishes his humanity. And as it is for men, so it is for nations.

Americans are generally a sensible people, and the wilder visions of the isolationists are unlikely to win out: people who use Norelco razors, watch Sony TVs, cook with Cuisinarts, and drive Volkswagens, Saabs, and Acuras are unlikely to buy the idea that America can, or should want to, escape the realities of an interlocked international economy. On the other hand, the disproportionate part of the burden of the common defense that Americans have borne for two generations may well have created a lassitude in the American body politic that will make it more susceptible to the argument that there is little America can or should do to shape the *politics* of nations, beyond taking the necessary steps to insure the physical security of the United States. But that, as President Václav Havel of Czechoslovakia made plain in his address to a joint session of the Congress, is not all that the world expects of the United States of America.

The claims made on American international activism—moral, cultural, economic, perhaps even military—by human rights advocates struggling against tyranny and by the new democracies of Latin America and east central Europe are really moral claims. They are the claims that democrats make on fellow democrats, and those claims in turn reflect a normative vision of decent human relationships that is, apparently, a universal cultural foundation of democratic politics. That normative vision finds its deepest taproots, I believe, in Jewish and Christian understandings of the human person, human society, human history and destiny. Whether we style those understandings "biblical religion" or "ethical monotheism," the point to be made is that the concepts of God as one, and as Creator and Father, preclude autarky as a morally satisfactory model of human relationships.

Defining a politics of post–Cold War internationalism that is proof against the utopian temptations that bedeviled presidents Wilson and Carter is no easy business. It requires a concept of man, and of politics, that is neither Pelagian nor Hobbesian. It requires a concept of international public life, and of the peace that is possible within that diverse environment, that is at once worldly (in the best sense of the term) and tethered to norms that transcend our immediate circumstances. It demands the ability to make finely tuned calculations about the times and places in which the proportionate and discriminate use of armed force can advance the cause of peace and freedom. It requires an appreciation of the power of moral force, as embodied by the non-violent revolutionaries of 1989. It requires a sense of personal moral obligation to others beyond our immediate national political community that is sufficiently grounded in a sense of mature patriotism that it does not drift off into the mists of "global citizenship."

Where might such an ethics of international politics be found?

I believe that, within the worlds of American ethics, both secular and religious, the classic Catholic moral understanding of international public life that I styled "the heritage of *tranquillitas ordinis*" constitutes as coherent, rational, and persuasive an ethical (and political) framework for thinking through our responsibilities and opportunities as we can find. Here we can discover a way to relate the national interest to a sense of international purpose. Here we find an answer to the question, "Why engage?" that is neither romantic nor demeaningly self-centered. Here, if we look carefully enough, we find idealism without illusions and realism without cynicism.

Tranquillitas ordinis is not "the brotherhood of man under the Fatherhood of God," as liberal Protestantism once understood the goal of Christian social ethical reflection and action. Its vision is more modest than that. But it is a vision of peace through freedom whose very modesty, as was so amply demonstrated by the Revolution of 1989, has a certain grandeur about it. The public debate along this internationalist/isolationist axis badly needs the richness of more texture that an extended and developed Catholic heritage could provide. Whether the Church in America will help provide it is, perhaps, the key test of whether American Catholics have indeed accepted the challenge of peace.

4

Camels and Needles, Talents and Treasure: American Catholicism and the Capitalist Ethic

"Where your treasure is, there will your heart be also."

—Matthew 6:21

"And Jesus said to his disciples, 'Truly, I say to you, it will be hard for a rich man to enter the kingdom of heaven. Again I tell you, it is easier for a camel to go through the eye of a needle than for a rich man to enter the kingdom of God.' When the disciples heard this they were greatly astonished, saying, 'Who then can be saved?' But Jesus looked at them and said to them, 'With men this is impossible, but with God all things are possible.' "

—Matthew 19:23–26

"[The kingdom of heaven] will be as when a man going on a journey called his servants and entrusted to them his property; to one he gave five talents, to another two, to another one, according to his ability. Then he went away. He who had received the five talents went at once and traded with them; and he made five talents more. . . . But he who had received the one talent went and dug in the ground and hid his master's money.

"Now after a long time the master of those servants came and settled accounts with them. And he who had received the five talents came forward, bringing five talents more, saying, 'Master, you delivered to me five talents; here I have made five talents more.' His master said to him, 'Well done, good and faithful servant; you have been faithful over a little, I will set you over much more; enter into the joy of your master.' . . . He also who had received the one talent came forward, saying, 'Master, I knew you to be a hard man . . . so I was afraid, and I went and hid your talent in the ground. Here is what is yours.' But his master answered him, 'You wicked and slothful servant! You knew that I reap where I have not sowed, and gather where I have not winnowed? Then you ought to have invested my money with the bankers, and at my coming I should have received what was my own with interest. . . . Cast the worthless servant into the outer darkness; there men will weep and gnash their teeth.' "

—Matthew 25:14–30

I magine yourself a successful, contemporary American Catholic businessman or woman. You have achieved a level of material prosperity of which your grandparents (who were probably immigrants) could only dream. Your faith, which you take seriously (probably far more seriously than your WASP or Jewish colleagues, although perhaps less intensely than your evangelical Protestant fellow entrepreneurs), is not an obstruction to your economic or social success and status, as it might have been a generation ago; on the contrary, you are regularly struck by the number of fellow Catholics whom you meet at the higher altitudes of CEO-dom. Your regular donations to the church and your secular philanthropic activities seem to be morally and spiritually legitimated by what you hear from the pulpit in your suburban parish on Sunday, and in the pastoral letters (and Annual Drive requests!) of your bishop. The occasional glance at the *National Catholic Reporter* notwithstanding, you do not experience any serious tension between your economic and social status and your Catholic commitment.

But what about your daily activities: do you hear or read anything from the religious leadership of your church that could be construed as a moral, theological, and spiritual legitimation of your efforts to create wealth? Your entrepreneurial energies have made jobs available to others. Your success has meant success—in investments, in employment, in personal satisfaction—for thousands of employees and shareholders. Through the tax system, and through your philanthropic activities, you are making a significant contribution to the common good. What does your Catholicism have to say about all *that*?

If the truth be told, not much at all. Why should this be so? Why does an ancient religious tradition, successfully inculturated in the United States and claiming that its social teaching and its various approaches to lay spirituality carry insights into the public dimension of human life, seem to have so little to say to the business world? Does something in the nature of Catholic social thought, as it has evolved over the past century, impede the development of an "ethic of wealth creation"? How have the special historical and sociological circumstances of Catholicism in the United States contributed to today's situation? Are there resources in the Catholic tradition, in its classical expressions as well as in its distinctively American experience, that might lend themselves to the development of an ethic of entrepreneurship and wealth creation, and to the definition of a lay spirituality for a society primarily characterized by abundance rather than poverty?

Perhaps the first of these questions is not entirely fair: did the sociological conditions for the possibility of an ethic of wealth creation exist in American Catholicism prior to, say, the late 1950s? Still, and given the massive empirical evidence that Catholics have, in the main, achieved success in the United States, one might think this achievement would have been sustained, in part, by a theology, ethics, and spirituality that gave it moral legitimacy. The very fact of that "success" suggests that there was nothing in the popular spirituality of pre-Conciliar American Catholicism that impeded Catholic economic energies. On the contrary, the Church's traditional emphasis on education, its legitimation of the bourgeois family, its stress on personal discipline (in the order of ideas and values), and its sundry formal and informal "networks" and support systems (in the order of institutions) undoubtedly played a significant role in the assimilation and economic success of the American Catholic community. But this popular spirituality was not buttressed by a theological and ethical rationale that could plausibly be termed an "ethic of wealth creation." Nor do contemporary American Catholic religious leaders and intellectual elites seem to feel any urgency about developing such an ethic. A brief look at some salient points of American Catholic history may help explain why.

PRE-1960s: AN URBAN,
WORKING-CLASS CHURCH

In 1776 there were only about 35,000 Catholics in the newly proclaimed United States (0.8% of the national population). They lived primarily in Maryland, with enclaves in New York, Pennsylvania, and the French settlements west of the Alleghenies. At the time of the Revolution, Catholics were still legally disenfranchised in Maryland, the colony founded in 1634 as a religious refuge for them. The leadership of this tiny community was firmly in the hands of "old Catholics" from the Maryland gentry like the Carroll family, whose two most prominent members were John Carroll, the first Catholic bishop in the United States, and Charles Carroll of Carrollton, the last surviving signer of the Declaration of Independence. At his death in 1832, Charles Carroll was also reputed to be the wealthiest single person in the United States.

Archbishop John Carroll's impressive efforts to bring some order and stability to Catholic life in the United States, and Charles Carroll's work (often in tandem with his episcopal cousin) to break through the barriers of anti-Catholic prejudice that continued to exist even after the Revolution, are beyond the scope of this essay.[1] What we should remember is that the Maryland-centered "old Catholics"—a gentry class whose spirituality was largely ordered to private devotion (given the paucity of clergy to lead public worship, and the dangers attendant thereon because of anti-Catholic bigotry)[2]—were quickly displaced by the waves of immigrants who, beginning in the early nineteenth century, soon engulfed and transformed the American Catholic community.

These new Catholic Americans, primarily Irish, were indeed the "wretched refuse" of the Old World. Desperately poor, usually illiterate, lacking the work skills and personal disciplines that were important elements of success in the early stages of the Industrial Revolution, the immigrants of the ante-bellum nineteenth century were a challenge of extraordinary proportions to the Church. That the challenge was, in the main, successfully met—that the laboring class in the United States was not lost to the Church as it was in Europe at that very time—remains one of the crowning glories of Catholicism in the United States. These were not, however, circumstances in which the development of a sophisticated ethic of wealth creation, or a spirituality of entrepreneurship, was likely. When a working-class church occasionally turned its attention beyond the neighborhood parish to the wider national economic and social scene, it would naturally reflect the concerns and perspectives of the working class.

Capitalism = Exploitation

This was particularly true of a Church led by someone like Archbishop "Dagger John" Hughes of New York.[3] Archbishop Hughes was a pugnacious Irish immigrant, and thus perhaps a suspect witness in matters related to perfidious Albion. But his lurid description of conditions in English society in 1844, in what he freely conceded was the richest country in the world, gives us some of the flavor (and argumentation) of ante-bellum American Catholic social thought, as well as an insight into the kind of modernity that Hughes (and doubtless other American Catholic leaders) wished to avoid in America:

> [England] has, indeed, fought the great battle for wealth with other countries and has, by universal consent, gained the victory. But how comes it that, while a few of her sons are rioting in the spoils of the vanquished, the cries of the wounded and dying of her own battalions are heard on every side? How comes it that in Ireland, out of a population between eight and nine millions, there are over two millions absolutely dependent on the charity of others, scarcely a degree above their own condition? How comes it that, in Scotland, misery and destitution are hardly less general, and, from other causes, perhaps even more excruciating still? How comes it that, in England itself, distress among the laboring classes presses, at intervals, to such an extreme point, as to threaten, from time to time, insurrection and revolution? How comes it, in fine, to happen that, while the dogs of landlords and capitalists are well fed and well housed—while their horses are daintily provided for, the sons and daughters of Britons around them go forth with gaunt looks and sunken features, through want of food?
>
> These are results which *puzzle* political economists, but which never could have happened, if Political Economy had not been

transferred from the Christian basis on which it was originally reared in that country, to the inadequate foundations of mere individual interest. I am willing, then, to ascribe to the Protestant religion, the credit of England's wealth; but her poverty, and the destitution of her millions, must, I insist upon it, be charged to the same account.[4]

Hughes's lecture reflected several prominent themes in ante-bellum American Catholic social thought: the romanticizing of the socioeconomic circumstances of the Middle Ages; the identification (which Hughes adopted from William Cobbett) of capitalism with Protestantism and, through Protestantism, with a radical individualism; the linking of the profit motive to greed and selfishness; the view that Protestantism had destroyed the traditional authorities of the *ancien régime*, which had instructed people on their charitable duties; and the insistence on Catholicism as the only possible foundation of a just and humane society ordered to the common good.

Hughes's concerns were shared by the lay intellectual Orestes Brownson, whose 1840 polemic against capitalism was, if anything, more strident than the archbishop's. Brownson inveighed against what he took to be the moral hypocrisies of his age: "The owner who is involved in the systematic exploitation of . . . poor laborers is frequently one of our respectable citizens; perhaps he is praised in the newspapers for his liberal donations to some charitable institution. He passes among us as a pattern of morality, and is honored as a worthy Christian."[5] These hypocrisies were the inevitable result of the class antagonisms that were endemic to capitalism: "It is for the interest of the trader to cheat—to buy under value and to sell over value; it is for the interest of the master to oppress the workman, by paying the least possible wages for the least (*sic*) possible amount of labor. This is the interest of one opposed to the interest of the other; and every man in pursuing his own interest must needs, as far as possible, overreach and supplant every other man."[6] The root of the evils of capitalism lay in the wage system: "Wages is a cunning device of the devil, for the benefit of tender consciences who would retain all the advantages of the slave system, without the experience, trouble, and odium of being slave-holders."[7] And, contrary to its nineteenth-century advocates, capitalism had made things worse rather than better: "The actual condition of the workingman today, viewed in all its bearings, is not so good as it was fifty years ago."[8]

Brownson shared Hughes's fondness for the Middle Ages (in which, he argued, there was less class antagonism than in antebellum America[9]), but he did not advocate a return to medieval social and economic patterns as such. Rather, "Brownson anticipated a reconstructed social order where the division between morality and politics and religion and economics was overcome in favor of a society where cooperation between brothers and sisters in pursuit of a common destiny was reflected in the halls of government and in the work places of America."[10] But as even the admiring John Mitchell has put it, delicately, "Brownson was unwilling to offer a detailed plan" for how this idealized and re-Christianized society might be constructed.[11]

There is nothing terribly original in Hughes's or Brownson's critiques; Hughes drew on Cobbett and Brownson on Thomas Carlyle for their portraits of working-class life and for their analyses of the causes of poverty. But we should note the anti-modernity strand in both Hughes and Brownson, and their seeming fondness for a monistic approach to questions of religion-and-society. Was the animus of Hughes and Brownson against capitalism per se, or against capitalism as the economic expression of modernization? And was this anti-modernity polemic fueled by an instinctive preference for a more intimate linkage between the Church and the society, the economy, and the polity—for monism rather than pluralism in the construction of the public order?

In any event, Hughes's and Brownson's war against capitalism—the sensibility that informed their critiques, the sociological situation from which they arose, the terms in which they were expressed themselves, the alternative models they seemed to favor—suggests that American Catholicism was in no condition to develop an "ethic of wealth creation" in the mid-nineteenth century. Distribution—or, more accurately, maldistribution—of wealth was the primary concern of church leaders when they turned their minds to matters economic.

The Question of Unions

After the Civil War, the most sustained ideological interaction between the formal leadership of the Church and the American economic system was on the question of trade unionism. Other issues, and some large-scale personalities, were also in play, complicating the picture in this period. These were the days in which Father Edward McGlynn was excommunicated for his advocacy of the economic and tax theories of Henry George,[12] while at just about the same time, Archbishop John Ireland had his new seminary in St. Paul built by robber baron James J. Hill.[13] However, trade unionism was the issue that would most influence the social thought of American Catholicism.

Archbishop Ireland's relationship with Hill, Cardinal James Gibbons's happy friendships with the leading families of Baltimore, and similar behavior by other major American Catholic leaders suggest that the late-nineteenth-century leadership of the Church was hostile neither to capitalism per se nor to capitalists as individuals. But given their primarily working-class constituency, and their determination that the debacle of European Catholicism in its loss of the working class not be repeated in the New World, it was only natural that the bishops' attention be focused on workers rather than on entrepreneurs, on labor rather than on capital.

The case that brought the labor issue to a head was the attempt, generated by conservative French Canadian bishops (with some help from members of the U.S. hierarchy in whose dioceses there had been violent strikes), to get the Vatican to condemn the Knights of Labor, a forerunner of modern trade-union federations. The Knights case was complicated by the organization's secrecy provisions (which were necessary for its functioning in those nasty days but to Roman eyes smacked of such condemned "secret societies" as the Masons), and by some of its leaders' support for Father McGlynn. To make a long and complex story drastically short,[14] the personal intervention of Cardinal Gibbons in Rome in 1887 prevented a Holy Office condemnation of the Knights, whose leadership at that time included a number of Catholics. (Interestingly enough, the Holy Office document allowing that the Knights could be "tolerated" also required that, in their constitution, "words which seem to favor socialism and communism must be amended in such a way as to make clear that the soil was granted by God to man, or rather the human race, that each one might have the right to acquire some portion of it, by use however of lawful means and without violation of the right of private property."[15])

Gibbons's intervention in the Knights of Labor controversy established a pattern of support between the American hierarchy and the American trade-union movement that continues to this day. While this support did not quite preclude the development of an ethic of wealth creation, it mitigated against it, again because of a primary focus on wealth distribution. One of the high points of the Church/labor connection was the 1919 "Bishops' Program for Social Reconstruction," issued in the wake of World War I. The program's proposals, which were condemned by the National Association of Manufacturers as "partisan, pro-labor-union, socialistic propaganda,"[16] became the agenda of the National Catholic Welfare Conference's social-action department during the inter-war period. Gerald Fogarty summarizes the Bishops' Program, the brainchild of Catholic University's professor of moral theology, Father John A. Ryan, in these terms:

> It called on the government to retain certain wartime agencies, notably the United States Employment Service and the National War Labor Board, which supported the rights to a living wage, to organized labor, and to collective bargaining. It asked for government loans to returning servicemen, for prevention of monopolies in commodities, for government regulation of monopolies of privately owned public services, and for heavy taxation of incomes and inheritances. It went on to propose government competition with private industry if anti-trust laws failed, wider distribution of stock among employees, the elimination of child labor through government taxation, and, while not favoring women in the labor force, equal pay for equal work for both men and women.[17]

Reactions to the Bishops' Program divided along ideological lines. Raymond Swing, writing in *The Nation*, thought that Father Ryan had produced something "better than anything produced by the AFL."[18] Conversely, a New York state senate committee investigating sedition claimed that the document came from "a certain group in the Catholic Church with leanings toward Socialism."[19] Much of this ideological cannonading became muted, of course, when the key provisions of the 1919 Program were written into law during Franklin Roosevelt's first administration (a development that earned Father—later Monsignor—Ryan the sobriquet "Right Reverend New Dealer"). For our purposes, however, the Bishops' Program is important as another signal that the times were not precisely right for the development of an "ethic of wealth creation" in American Catholicism. The focus remained, through the Great Depression and World War II, on the ethics of distribution, not creation.

The same focus is apparent in the Roman documents of the period. Dennis McCann is indulging in a bit of hyperbole when he characterizes Pope Leo XIII, author of *Rerum Novarum*, the Magna Carta of modern Catholic social thought, as "a dispossessed Italian prince unable to come to terms with the final disappearance of a feudal, agrarian society even in Central Europe."[20] Still, it is certainly true that *Rerum Novarum* was no radical document. Its endorsement of trade unionism was perhaps its most progressive feature, but the encyclical also went to great lengths to defend the rights of private property against socialism and communism, which Leo XIII seemed to find more immediately threatening than capitalism. On the other hand, McCann is surely right in saying that Leo held no brief for "the capitalist ethic," and would probably have regarded the term as oxymoronic.

Official Roman nervousness about capitalism (which, again, is not altogether easy to disentangle from official Roman nervousness about modernization in general during this period) is also evident in the great social encyclical of Pius XI, *Quadragesimo Anno* (1931), whose corporatism was posed as a "third way" between capitalism and communism. Official Roman social teaching found both the market and the commissars deficient in religious and moral grounding, and seemed to regard this deficiency as inherent in both instances. Here, too, was unfertile soil in which to expect an "ethic of wealth creation" to develop.

The Catholic discussion of political economy was complexified by the Second Vatican Council, whose tripartite discussion of modern society in *Gaudium et Spes* (the 1965 "Pastoral Constitution on the Church in the Modern World") anticipated later commentators' analysis of "democratic capitalism" as a system involving a market-oriented economy, a liberal democratic polity, and a pluralistic culture.[21] However, the Council's economics again stressed issues of distribution over issues of wealth creation, paid far more attention to labor than to entrepreneurship, and analyzed the difficulties of the Third World in terms of what the council fathers believed was the growing gap between rich and poor.[22] This last theme would become even more prominent in Pope Paul VI's 1968 encyclical *Populorum Progressio*, a document notable for its pronounced prejudice against capitalist forms of development.[23] As in the late nineteenth and early twentieth centuries, the mid-century Roman discussion of political economy gave little impetus to the development in American Catholicism of an ethic of wealth creation.

Such a development was further impeded by the influence in post-Conciliar American Catholicism of those Latin American theologies of liberation whose animus toward market-oriented economies made Paul VI look virtually Manchesterian by comparison.[24] The North American ground for the reception of liberation theology had already been prepared, in activist and intellectual circles, by the Catholic Worker movement, whose founders, Peter Maurin and Dorothy Day, emphasized, respectively, corporatist and anarchist approaches to issues of politics and economics—the common thread between these two rather divergent views being a profound distaste for capitalism.[25]

Post-1960s: A Suburban, Middle-Class Church

If ideas have a social location—if they require a favorable climate and soil in which to take root and grow—then from what we have seen so far there was little reason to expect American Catholicism to have evolved a theology, ethics, and spirituality of entrepreneurship prior to World War II, and indeed prior to the 1960s. Before that decade, American Catholics were overwhelmingly working-class; their economic concerns were with wealth distribution, not wealth creation.

Contemporary American Catholics live in far different economic and social conditions than their parents and grandparents. The American Catholic Church is still a heavily immigrant Church; 25 per cent of German-American and Irish-American Catholics, 52 per cent of Polish-American Catholics, and 72 per cent of Italian-American Catholics are either foreign-born or first-generation Americans. These sons and daughters of immigrants have done spectacularly well. American Catholics are second in family income to American Jews, and thus ahead of American Episcopalians, Presbyterians, Methodists, Lutherans, and Baptists. American Catholics, as a whole, are even with the national averages in educational attainment and occupational prestige; and the older immigrants, the German-American and Irish-American Catholics, are above the average on these indices.[26] Given these data, the classic nativist canard, that the Catholic tradition would create obstacles to Catholics' full participation in American economic, social, and political life, seems even more absurd than ever (its occasional reappearances on the editorial page of the *New York Times* notwithstanding). In fact, as suggested above, there may well be distinctively Catholic habits of mind and institutional circumstances that favored Catholic accomplishment in America.

A Missed Opportunity

Changed demographic circumstances ought to have led to changed attitudes. The rapid and dramatic transformation of American Catholicism in the post-war period from an urban, working-class Church to a Church of the suburban middle- and upper-middle classes created the sociological conditions required for a theology, ethics, and spirituality of wealth creation to develop. Indeed, some probes have been made in that direction.[27] But they are just that, probes, and their makers are regarded with attitudes ranging from faint amusement to barely disguised contempt by the current American Catholic intellectual establishment.

Why has this happened? The answer again lies in the social location of ideas. Parallel to the rise of what we might call the Catholic CEO class over the past generation, a new class of Catholic intellectuals and publicists has developed. These people are highly influential (through the prominent Catholic opinion journals, through seminaries and universities) and are bureaucratically well positioned (at both the diocesan and the national level, and in religious communities), and they bear a standard "new class" animus toward the old business-class elite—which now just happens to be composed, in significant part, of the Catholic new class's co-religionists.[28]

Those who appreciate Peter Rossi's *mot* that there are many ironies in the fire will doubtless find confirmation for the ironic view of history in this situation: that, at the precise moment when the socioeconomic conditions in American Catholicism were ripe for the development of an ethic of wealth creation, the main intellectual and opinion switchboards in the American Church were in the hands of a new class of intellectuals and activists whose attitudes toward capitalism were, at best, frosty. Others will find in this situation a confirmation of their judgment that capitalism's great weakness is its seeming inability to generate persuasive and evocative "myths" that legitimate its empirically undeniable material successes: and then the argument will proceed as to whether this is an "intrinsic incapacity" (*pace* Peter Berger) or the result of lack of attention to the problem (*pace* Michael Novak). Be *that* argument as it may, whatever the cause, the fact remains that the current sociological openness to the development of an ethic of wealth creation in American Catholicism is being actively impeded by the emergence of the Catholic new class, whose anti-capitalist bias is scarcely less vehement than that of John Hughes or Orestes Brownson.[29]

"Economic Justice for All"

The tension between the facts of American Catholic economic and social achievement, on the one hand, and the ideological biases of the American Catholic new class, on the other, was one dynamic in the production of the American bishops' 1986 national pastoral letter, *Economic Justice for All*. The process leading to the letter began with a motion at the 1980 annual meeting of the National Conference of Catholic Bishops. That meeting had adopted a well-argued (though singularly ignored) *Pastoral Letter on Marxist Com-*

munism, and Hartford auxiliary bishop Peter Rosazza proposed that the bishops devote a pastoral letter to capitalism, in order to be "balanced."[30] Bishop Rosazza's motion was accepted, and the mandate of the drafting committee was expanded to include the full range of issues involved in American economic life.

Like the bishops' 1983 letter, *The Challenge of Peace*, *Economic Justice for All* had a specific historical focus: the Reagan administration, and all its works, and all its array. Reagan administration rhetoric and policy on nuclear weapons and strategy had been influential (some would say determinative) in motivating the bishops to issue *The Challenge of Peace*,[31] and similar vectors of influence were doubtless at work in shaping *Economic Justice for All*, which, viewed from one angle, is a principled and lengthy objection to the supply-side revolution.

This is not the place to analyze *Economic Justice for All* in detail. Suffice it to say that the pastoral letter did little to advance the development of an ethic of wealth creation in American Catholicism. The pastoral's biblical section, though it begins with a brief reflection on divine creativity in the world, is primarily focused on the virtue of justice, understood largely in terms of distributive justice.[32] The pastoral's exhortations are addressed to "blue collar workers, managers, homemakers, politicians, and others,"[33] but not entrepreneurs. The bishops write that they wish to "encourage and support a renewed sense of vocation in the business community,"[34] but that vocation is never discussed in terms of the creation of wealth.

It may well be, as John Langan, S.J., has argued, that *Economic Justice for All* is "more accepting of the patterns of U.S. capitalism than are standard presentations of Catholic social thought as a middle ground or third way between capitalism and socialism."[35] The pastoral is not actively hostile to the development of an ethic and spirituality of entrepreneurship; but such a development is not among the various urgent items on its ecclesial agenda. In this respect, at least, the 1986 pastoral letter represents a culmination of the pattern of missed opportunity that has unfolded in recent years under the influence of a new-class intellectual elite hostile toward market-oriented economies and the business class.[36]

ELEMENTS OF AN ETHIC OF
WEALTH CREATION

Materials are not lacking for the development of a Catholic ethic of wealth creation with special resonance in the United States. Among the ample resources to be tapped are the following:

1. *The creation-centered social thought of John Paul II.*

Catholic socialists acclaim John Paul II for leading an alleged opening to the Left.[37] This interpretation of the encyclicals *Laborem Exercens* and *Sollicitudo Rei Socialis* is shared (minus the acclaim, of course) by some Catholic conservatives.[38] Although it is true that the pope's personal preferences seem to lie in the direction of some sort of social democracy (an inclination he shares with many other northern and eastern European intellectuals), John Paul's most distinctive contribution to the development of modern Catholic social thought has been in a decidedly entrepreneurial direction, in his identification (in *Sollicitudo*) of a "right of economic initiative."[39]

The pope's definition of this right is located within that creation-centered theology of the person to which he devoted considerable attention in his inaugural encyclical, *Redemptor Hominis*, and which forms the foundation of his theology of work in *Laborem Exercens*. In the latter, for example, the pope writes, "The word of God's revelation is profoundly marked by the fundamental truth that man, created in the image of God, shares by his work in the activity of the creator and that, within the limits of his own human capabilities, man in a sense continues to develop that activity, and perfects it as he advances further and further in the discovery of the resources and values contained in the whole of creation."[40]

In *Sollicitudo*, the pope takes the discussion an important step further by identifying "economic initiative" (what others might term "entrepreneurship" or "wealth creation") with "the creative subjectivity of the citizen"—a reflection in history and society of the divine creativity that began and sustains this world. Wealth creation, in this analysis, is a specifically economic form of human participation in God's abiding creativity, God's sustaining care for his creation.[41]

Writing prior to the publication of *Sollicitudo*, the Lay Commission on Catholic Social Teaching and the U.S. Economy suggested that the Roman magisterium had not paid adequate attention to entrepreneurship as an expression of human creativity "under God":

> Catholic social thought has not yet put sufficient emphasis upon the creative instrument through which new ideas and inventions are brought into service to human beings: the practical insight of the entrepreneur. By themselves, brilliant ideas do not serve humankind; to be brought into service to man, they must be transformed through complex processes of design and production. The talent to perform this transformation is as rare and humanly precious as talent in any other field. Indeed, the promotion of entrepreneurial talent is indispensable if the "cry of the poor" is to be heard. If not the man or woman of enterprise, who else will create new wealth? Who else will invent new opportunities for employment?[42]

It would be going rather too far to claim that *Sollicitudo Rei Socialis* clearly identifies entrepreneurship as the key to economic justice for all; but the pope's endorsement of the "right of economic initiative" does suggest that the Roman magisterium is more open to the moral case for democratic capitalism than it has ever been in the past—and such an openness is the prerequisite to a moral legitimation of entrepreneurship. Moreover, the pope's locating of this "right" within the framework of his creation-centered theology of the human person ought to be attractive to Americans, taught by Jefferson that "the God who gave us life, gave us liberty, at the same time."

2. The "preferential option for the poor."

This ubiquitous formulation (which Peter Berger once described as sounding like "a bad English translation of a bad Spanish translation of a bad German idea") is generally taken to be the slogan of those who would look last (if at all) to capitalism, entrepreneurship, and economic initiative as the means toward economic justice for all. Conversely, the tendency of those of us who look precisely to the capitalist revolution for the effective pursuit of that morally desirable end is usually to abandon the phrase and even the concept of a "love of preference for the poor" (in Cardinal Joseph Ratzinger's reformulation). This is, I think, a mistake.

It is a mistake, first, because the "preferential option" language has become embedded in the contemporary Catholic discourse, even at the official level,[43] and no amount of kvetching seems likely to dislodge it in the foreseeable future. The "preferential option" or "love of preference" for the poor is here to stay. And matters of euphony notwithstanding, the real issue is the content that is put into the phrase.

Second, it is a mistake for the entrepreneurially oriented to assume that the "preferential option" must necessarily involve a state-centered or market-deprecating approach to economic life and social change. This, argues Dennis McCann, is not what the American bishops had in mind when they endorsed the preferential option in *Economic Justice for All*. Their letter, McCann suggests, treats the preferential option in formal terms as a "middle axiom" whose substantive content is primarily evangelical rather than political or economic. "The option for the poor is clearly meant to be imitative of Christ's way of acting," writes McCann; but it does not call the Church into class struggle, it does not confer a "hermeneutic privilege" (that is, a greater ability to discern the truth) on those whose incomes fall below a certain level, and it does not necessarily drive Catholic social thought away from market-oriented approaches to economic development and empowerment.[44] In their endorsement of the preferential option, the American bishops "are defining a moral litmus test for a just society that is both an authentic reflection of the religious vision animating Catholic social teaching and an appropriate expression of our common moral aspirations as Americans"[45]—nothing less than that, but nothing more, either.

McCann rightly notes that his interpretation of the bishops' use of "preferential option" will be disappointing to "partisans of liberation theology"; but it ought to be attractive to those who are convinced, first, that there is no way around the formulation in the contemporary Catholic debate, and second, that entrepreneurship, enterprise, and economic initiative—capitalism, in other words— are the instruments most likely to help the poor get out of poverty. For if the preferential option is a middle axiom, whose function is to be understood formally, then the substantive debate remains wide open, and the question of precisely how to exercise the option can be argued on grounds favorable to those who would press the capitalist case, namely, the empirical grounds sketched by Peter Berger in *The Capitalist Revolution*.[46]

Economic Justice for All—and its guiding middle axiom, the "preferential option for the poor"—can thus, with a bit of hermeneutic judo, become an ally in the evolution of an American Catholic ethic of wealth creation.

3. The social analysis of Jacques Maritain.

Ralph McInerny, rereading Jacques Maritain's *Reflections on America* some thirty years after its original publication in 1958, was struck by the Frenchman's thoughts about American capitalism. In his *Integral Humanism*, Maritain had taken a rather hostile attitude toward capitalism as a system "grounded on the principle of the fecundity of money and the absolute primacy of individual profit"; but in America, that hotbed of capitalist enterprise, Maritain discovered a people who "were freedom-loving and mankind-loving . . . , people clinging to the importance of ethical standards, anxious to save the world, the most humane and the least materialist among modern peoples which had reached the industrial age."[47]

America was not a materialistic nation; there was "no avarice in the American cast of mind." Americans frankly recognized that money was important, and this disturbed some Europeans; but, Maritain argued, "the ordinary course of American institutions and the innumerable American private groups show us that the ancient Greek and Roman idea of the *civis praeclarus*, the dedicated citizen who spends his money in the service of the common good, plays an essential part in the American consciousness." The notion of American materialism, Maritain concluded, was "no more than a curtain of silly gossip and slander."[48]

It is striking that *Economic Justice for All*, a document whose notes refer to Richard Barnet, Gar Alperovitz, Michael Harrington, and E. F. Schumacher, among others, did not find occasion to mention *Reflections on America*. Charity, and the possibility of the hermeneutic judo suggested above, forbid speculation as to why. But any ethic of wealth creation in American Catholicism is going to have to confront, in addition to the drumbeat of new-class criticism about American greed, Maritain's claim that American materialism is, at the very least, of a very distinctive sort. The development of such an ethic will include careful reflection on current patterns of philanthropy and private charitable giving in the United States, taking the good news, that personal and corporate giving has risen throughout the 1980s, along with the bad, that today's American Catholics, despite their economic advantages, are giving to their Church far less generously than their parents and grandparents.

Other Points to Consider

An emerging American Catholic ethic of wealth creation should also address the following concerns:

1. *Leisure*. A classically grounded Catholic ethic of wealth creation will have to confront, and might well incorporate, the analysis of Josef Pieper in his *Leisure: The Basis of Culture*.[49] The simple-minded may regard Pieper's work as reflecting the kind of Catholic lassitude and lack of interest in the real world of commerce that was overcome by the northern European Protestant ethic during the Industrial Revolution. Pieper's book, however, does not so much argue against the work ethic as attempt to locate that ethic within a broader cultural horizon so that the question "Work for what?" gets due attention. Work, as John Paul II has insisted, is an expression of human creativity, and man works in order to "elevate increasingly the cultural and moral level of the society in which he lives in community with those who belong to the same family." Moreover, human beings exercise their divinely mandated creativity in a dialectic of work and leisure: "Man ought to imitate God both in working and also in resting, since God himself wished to present his own creative activity under the form of work and rest."[50] The world of work is not a more real world than the world of leisure; rather, work and leisure are two moments in the unfolding dialectic of human creativity under God.

This classic Catholic discussion may have a particular relevance for the contemporary American scene in view of the plethora of books and conferences urging the United States to be more like Japan because "Japan is number one." "More like Japan" usually means more ruthlessly meritocratic and hierarchical; more locked into the notion of work and wealth creation as ends in themselves, with little or no connection to the world of leisure; more, to use an otherwise troubling neologism from the modern Roman magisterium, "economistic." Perhaps those characteristics of modern Japanese society give Japan a comparative advantage in some aspects of international trade and finance; but it is not at all self-evident that America must, or indeed should, imitate such characteristics, since they seem to involve other cultural trade-offs that we may not wish to make. In any event, Pieper's analysis of leisure and culture, and John Paul II's dialectic of work and rest, ought to be incorporated into the discussion of an American Catholic ethic of wealth creation, on their own merits and as an antidote to that new form of works righteousness that marches under the banner "Japan is number one."

2. *Spirituality and vocation.* An ethic of wealth creation will have to address the question of spirituality in a society of abundance. Chesterton's observation that "there is more simplicity in the man who eats caviar on impulse that in the man who eats grape-nuts on principle" may give little comfort to the health faddists among us (and that in itself is no small recommendation for GKC's insight); but it reminds us that interior disposition is at least as significant a dimension of the spiritual life as external practice—a Christian understanding with a long pedigree, dating back to the parable of the Pharisee and the publican (Luke 18:9–14).

Gilbert Meilaender has identified three dispositions, each with an honorable history in Christian thought, toward possessions:

1. Possessions are both a dangerous threat and a good opportunity. To avoid the dangers, we need the virtue of *simplicity*—to choke off the passion for things and moderate our desires. To seize the opportunities for service, we need the virtue of *generosity*.

2. Regularly seizing the opportunity to give to those in need may call for and give rise to something more than a moderation of our desires; it may suggest the need for *renunciation*. Clement [of Alexandria] writes to oppose this move, and he is surely correct to see that not all Christians are called to such a life— correct also to see that this is no higher life, since it can offer no

guarantee of a purer inner spirit. What Jesus says to the rich ruler is the precise truth: *no one* is good but God alone. . . .

3. An attempt to practice the virtues of simplicity and generosity may give rise to a sense of *tension* within the Christian life—tension that pushes the whole of that life in a relatively *austere* direction. Presupposing the possession of goods, the virtue of generosity seems . . . to call simply for a right inner spirit and by itself sets no limit (other than the neighbor's need) to what we possess. Presupposing the danger of possessions, the virtue of simplicity reminds us that things are not simply neutral. Too much—though also too little—can corrupt the soul.[51]

There is no simple answer to the related questions of interior disposition and public practice in this matter of wealth, its uses, and its temptations. But Meilaender's reflections on what we might call the "tug toward austerity" in classic Christian spirituality should not be taken as antipathetic toward an ethic of wealth creation, particularly if that ethic is lived out in a vocationally serious effort to serve others. Wealth creation need not, in other words, result in its creators' becoming self-aggrandizing wastrels. Not all entrepreneurs are Donald Trump, and no serious Christian entrepreneur will find his vocational compass oriented toward conspicuous consumption.

Meilaender also reminds us that austerity is not a good in and of itself. We can, writes Meilaender, "retreat from the life of society; we may choose subsistence for ourselves"; but to do that is also to retreat "from a life of exchange and interdependence into a life of autonomy and independence." Such a retreat is no guarantee of virtue, and quite possibly as much a threat to it as the temptations of over-consumption.

The key to public Christian life within the tension Meilaender identifies—the tension between the parable of the talents and Jesus' saying about camels and needles—may well lie in one's willingness to live a vocational, as distinguished from careerist, life. Not all Christians, not all Catholics, are called to be entrepreneurs and creators of wealth; but some surely are, and in living that vocation as a matter of service to others, the entrepreneur is participating in that godly creativity which is man's distinguishing characteristic. Some Christians are, conversely, called to a life of service to others and austerity, even radical austerity; but that call is not, by itself, a ticket to spiritual eminence. For some it may well be; for others it can lead to the worst forms of pride and hubris.

Meilaender's summary statement is important for those interested in developing an ethic of wealth creation, and ought to be pondered as well by those who regard such a project as inherently inferior in vocational terms:

> Room must be left for freedom of the Christian life—and, perhaps still more, freedom of the God who calls Christians to different ways of life. Beneficence to others in need is a duty for all Christians, but the ways in which that beneficence may be enacted are many, and no single way can be universally required.[52]

CONCLUDING OBSERVATIONS

In the theological core of Roman Catholic social thought there is nothing that precludes the development of an ethic of wealth creation, and much that might in fact point toward it. Contemporary Catholic theology's emphasis on the analogous relationship between divine and human creativity (as developed by the Karol Wojtyla, not the Matthew Fox, wing of the Church!) is one important theological foundation for the development of such an ethic. The classic Catholic social ethical principle of subsidiarity, which, among other things, seeks to set boundaries on the pretensions of the modern state, would also seem to favor entrepreneurial and market-oriented approaches to economics, rather than state-centered or central-planning models. So, too, would the parallel social ethical principle of personalism, particularly when the personalism in question emphasizes the virtue of creativity. In *Sollicitudo Rei Socialis*, we may indeed see the beginnings of a move toward the moral legitimation, indeed celebration, of some forms of entrepreneurship on the part of the Roman magisterium.

On the other hand, it should be frankly admitted that such a move will involve a kind of development of social doctrine, for much in the economic and political analysis of the classics of modern Catholic social thought—particularly *Quadragesimo Anno* and *Populorum Progressio*—points in a rather different direction. Whether that is the result of an anti-capitalist bias per se, or the reflection of more generalized Roman concerns about modernization, is a question worth further exploration. That exploration will be complicated by the fact that there is a concerted effort under way, by publicists such as Gregory Baum in Canada and Dale Vree in the United States, to claim John Paul II's social teaching for the democratic socialist camp. That effort, however implausible it may appear, will reinforce the problems for an evolving ethic of wealth creation posed by the generally anti-capitalist animus of the American Catholic new class.

Still, there is more "readiness" for such an evolution in contemporary American Catholicism than at any other time in our history. The immigrant Church of the working class has been transformed into the suburban Church of the middle and upper-middle class. That transformation, which is not without its difficulties and tensions, creates the sociological conditions needed for the development of an ethic of wealth creation in American Catholicism. Whether that opportunity will be seized—for the benefit of the poor, as well as for the moral legitimation of the entrepreneurs—is another question.

PART THREE

The Life of the Mind

5

The Ecumenism of Time: American Catholic Intellectual Life Today

A BRIEF PROLOGUE, IN LITURGICAL FORM. The texts for to-day are taken from *The Habit of Being: Letters of Flannery O'Connor*.

The First Lesson:

One of the awful things about writing when you are a Chris-tian is that for you the ultimate reality is the Incarnation, the present reality is the Incarnation, the whole reality is the Incarnation. . . .

For me a dogma is only a gateway to contemplation and is an instrument of freedom and not of restriction.[1]

The Second Lesson:

Fr. de Menacse told somebody not to come into the Church until he felt it would be an enlargement of his freedom. . . . I suppose it is like marriage, that when you get into it, you find it is the beginning, not the end, of the struggle to make love work. . . .

I couldn't make any judgment on the *Summa*, except to say this: I read it every night before I go to bed. If my mother were to come in during this process and say, "Turn off that light. It's late," I with lifted finger and broad bland beatific expression, would reply, "On the contrary, I answer that the light, being eternal and limitless, cannot be turned off. Shut your eyes," or some such thing. In any case I feel I can personally guarantee that St. Thomas loved God because for the life of me I cannot help loving St. Thomas. His brothers didn't want him to waste himself being a Dominican and so locked him up in a tower and introduced a prostitute into his apartment; her he ran out with a red-hot poker. It would be fashionable to be in sympathy with the woman, but I am in sympathy with St. Thomas.[2]

The Third Lesson:

I was once, five or six years ago, taken by some friends to have dinner with Mary McCarthy and her husband, Mr. Broadwater. . . . She departed the Church at the age of fifteen and is a Big Intellectual. We went at eight and at one, I hadn't opened my mouth once, there being nothing for me in such company to say. . . . Having me there was like having a dog present who had been trained to say a few words but overcome with inadequacy had forgotten them. Well, toward morning, the conversation turned on the Eucharist, which I, being the Catholic, was obviously supposed to defend. Mrs. Broadwater said when she was a child and received the Host, she thought of it as the Holy Ghost, He being the "most portable" person of the Trinity; now she thought of it as a symbol and implied that it was a pretty good one. I then said, in a very shaky voice, "Well, if it's a symbol, to hell with it." That was all the defense I was capable of but I realize now that this is all I will ever be able to say about it, outside of a story, except that it is the center of existence for me; all the rest of life is expendable.[3]

The Homily:

We don't have very many people in American Catholicism who write things like that, or write like that, anymore—which has to do with something more than the fact that Mary Flannery O'Connor was a rare spirit of the kind a community cannot manufacture, but can only receive and nurture. In another sense, it has something to do with the present state and future prospects of Catholic intellectual life in America. Is the intellectual life of American Catholicism today such that it could recognize, let alone nurture and sustain, some nascent Flannery O'Connor?[4]

Unless we can answer yes—and do so without romanticizing the Catholic Fifties, without denigrating the intellectual accomplishments of the past generation, and without losing the special character of the endeavor suggested by the notion of *Catholic* intellectual life—then we are indeed in trouble.

SECULARIZATION THEORY, R.I.P.

Few ideas have so dominated American Catholic intellectual life since the early 1960s as what is generally referred to as the "secularization hypothesis." Simply put, the argument is that modernization inevitably and inexorably leads to the secularization of society and culture. The hypothesis comes in two forms. In the hard form, modernization leads to a radical secularization that means the "death of God" and the emergence of "religionless" Christianity. In the modified form, modernization creates a supermarket of beliefs and values-systems in which classic Christianity will be one product among many others, and with an indeterminate shelf-life.

In one way or another, though, the notion that America is the furnace of modernity and is therefore an increasingly secularized society has become a kind of unquestioned first principle among many—even most—American Catholic intellectuals.[5] The Catholics are not alone here, of course; the modernity = secularization equation is pandemic throughout the American academy. But the secularization hypothesis has had a particularly dramatic effect on those modern Catholic intellectuals who often seem to think they stand indicted before the bar of what Miss O'Connor would call the "Big Intellectuals," which is a dramatic role-reversal indeed.[6]

To say this is not to yearn and pine for some kind of intellectual "rollback," as seems to be envisioned by those Catholic "restorationists" for whom everything since Descartes has been pretty much a disaster. The scientific revolutions whose hallmarks are names such as Galileo, Copernicus, and Einstein and events such as the codification of the human genetic code; the philosophical revolution occasioned by the Cartesian "turn to the subject" and the Kantian critique of knowledge; the revolutions in the understanding of human society and the human psyche led by Durkheim, Weber, and Marx, Freud and Jung; the revolution in our understanding of the past that has come out of the development of the historical-critical method of reading ancient texts—these revolutions are part of the universal intellectual patrimony of mankind and, as such, grist for the Catholic intellectual mill.

But cannot one make the case that what Pope John XXIII and the Fathers of the Second Vatican Council intended as a *dialogue* between Catholicism and modern intellectual life has become something of a monologue? Have Catholic intellectuals opened the windows of the Church to the modern world, but failed to open the windows of modernity to the worlds of which it is a part?[7] Where today is the publicly engaged Catholic intellectual who, fully cognizant of the great Karl Rahner's seminal research on the nature of "symbol," will yet say, of the Eucharist (or the Incarnation) and to the Mary McCarthys of today, "Well, if it's a symbol, to hell with it"?

Many Catholic intellectuals seem to find such bluntness a trifle embarrassing. We are great qualifiers, we modern American Catholic intellectuals. Were we to find ourselves in a wee-hours-of-the-morning discussion about central Catholic truth claims with the "cultured despisers of religion," our culturally conditioned (and now intellectually justified, with great panache) instinct would be to be . . . understanding. We don't want to be offensive.[8] We know, now, how to talk about the historically contingent nature of dogmatic statements. We might refer our interlocutors to Father Richard McBrien's *Catholicism* for a host of opinions on just as many subjects. These are not bad things, in and of themselves. No doubt many have been brought to the faith, or brought back to the faith, or made less automatically dismissive of the faith, by modern Catholic intellectuals who have learned to listen, and to make distinctions, and not to press too hard.

I have no wish to return to the days of the theological manuals, with their ready-made answers to questions large and small. But it seems to me that something has been lost when important leaders in the American Catholic community of intellectual discourse seem to feel a profound discomfort with the assertion that "dogma . . . is an instrument of freedom and not of restriction." And is there not something worrisome about Catholic intellectuals who seem to spend the bulk of their professional energies in a deconstructive exercise to determine how little one has to believe, or do (or not do), in order to be a Catholic? Naming names is not my purpose here; but I think we ought to concede that the temptation to deconstruct the Catholic classics (in David Tracy's happy formulation[9]) runs strong in virtually all of us. No doubt, of course, that what some Catholic "restorationists" think of as "dogma" needs to be deconstructed. But when the historical-critical method and more radical efforts at deconstruction become a kind of end in themselves, rather than a set of (very limited) means to the end of securing the evangelical and community-forming character of dogma, then something has gone awry.[10]

A Hypothesis Without Evidence

It is beyond my scope here to trace in full the complex intellectual paths by which the necessary Catholic dialogue with modernity has become, in some cases, a monologue on the deconstruction of the classic Catholic (and catholic) theological tradition. But I might suggest that one intellectual impulse in this unhappy process has been a rather uncritical acceptance of the secularization hypothesis, which in these United States has everything going for it except the evidence.

Whatever else can be said about secularization theory—and I grant that it illuminates much of the recent history of the West—it has not been empirically confirmed in the United States. Quite the contrary: by no available empirical test can the American people be characterized as "secular," if the adjective is taken to mean tone-deaf to transcendently grounded religious belief. According to the relevant survey research, 90 per cent of the American people believe in God; 86 per cent believe that the Bible is "the inspired word of God"; 60 per cent pray daily and 75 per cent weekly; 57 per cent are formal members of a religious organization; 45 + per cent attend religious services weekly; and 25 per cent do regular voluntary work for a religious organization. Moreover (and of particular interest to educators in the "private" sector), Americans contributed somewhere between $40 and $50 *billion* to religious institutions in calendar 1987.

There are, of course, lies, damned lies, and statistics. But there is no way to conclude from these data that the American people have become tone-deaf to transcendent religion. Whatever may be the

case elsewhere, modernization has emphatically *not* meant secularization in the United States.[11]

Tired Blood in Mainline Protestantism

Furthermore, and on the evidence analyzed by Wade Clark Roof
and William McKinney in their recent study *American Mainline
Religion: Its Changing Shape and Future*, the churches that make
more stringent doctrinal and moral demands on their people are
the ones that are growing, while the churches of cultural accommodation—the churches of the Protestant mainline/oldline—continue to bleed congregants. The reasons for this situation are
complex and various, but Roof and McKinney offer one intriguing
causal analysis that bears reflection:

> Today these churches are sometimes described as "old-line"—
> largely because of their once historic significance and currently
> declining influence. Declines in institutional membership and
> support and a diminished influence since the 1960s point to a
> significant loss of vitality, more so for this sector of American
> religion than for any other. The self-confidence and aggressive-
> ness with which they once engaged the culture is now missing.
> Optimism about the country and democratic faith, and belief
> that American progress and prosperity are linked with the work
> of God in history—once marks of liberal theology—have all
> faded. Commitment to social action has remained important, yet
> not without exacting a spiritual price; concerns for personal faith
> and the cure of souls are judged by many to be neglected in the
> pursuit of other causes. *Having made more accommodations to
> modernity than any other major religious tradition*, liberal Protes-
> tantism shows many signs of tired blood: levels of orthodox
> belief are low, doubt and uncertainty in matters of faith common,
> knowledge of the Scriptures exceedingly low. A loss of morale
> and mission shows up in both its public demeanor and its
> corporate life.[12]

Or, to paraphrase a prominent Baptist minister, the path of mono-
logue-with-modernity might be said to go from the mainline to the
oldine to the sideline.

Has the decline of the hegemony of the liberal Protestant
churches been a result of their "putting the edge back onto the

Gospel," as some church political activists would have it? Perhaps, in some fairly isolated cases of personal disaffection. But since the new "edge" has more often than not had to do with such "reforms" as pro-Sandinista politics, wedding services for homosexuals,[13] and various forms of pantheism masquerading as environmental concern,[14] it seems more plausible that Roof and McKinney are right: mainline/oldline Protestantism is in dire straits because its leadership has become a chaplaincy to cultural chic as defined by the one part of the American population that is undoubtedly secularized— the "new class" cultural elite in the academy, the prestige press, and the popular entertainment industry.[15] This is not, to be gentle, a position from which it is altogether easy to present oneself as the herald of classic Christianity in any of its great Protestant forms: Lutheran, Calvinist, Anglican, or Wesleyan.

Mainline Protestantism is certainly not finished as a cultural force in America. Recent conferences of the Methodist and Presbyterian churches have shown considerable doctrinal seriousness, and the various official bilateral ecumenical dialogues continue to produce impressive theological work. But the history of mainline Protestantism since World War II ought to be read as an important cautionary tale for American Catholics, and especially for the intellectuals among them. The unwillingness of American Catholic theologians to be a self-disciplining professional community (as in the case of Fr. Matthew Fox); the eagerness of American Catholic feminist intellectuals to find an ongoing place in their deliberations for Mary Daly, who has self-consciously placed herself outside the tradition of the Christian classics;[16] concepts of academic freedom that tend to confirm the hoary nativist charge that "Catholic intellectual life" is an oxymoron, and that make it difficult to distinguish a Catholic institution in even the broadest sense of the term;[17] the ideological bias on social and political questions that I have analyzed elsewhere[18]—these straws in the wind suggest that the patterns of cultural accommodation that Roof and McKinney find to be a crucial element in the decline of the great Protestant mainline have important parallels in modern American Catholic intellectual life. And as the root of the Protestant decay lay, in considerable part, in the uncritical acceptance of secularization theory as the paradigm for understanding the American cultural situation,[19] it is essential that American Catholic intellectuals assess the degree to which a similar acquiescence has skewed their own perceptions, and thus the ways in which they place their tradition and its classics into dialogue with American culture.[20]

JOHN TRACY ELLIS REVISITED

No examination of American Catholic intellectual life can fail to grapple with the analysis proposed some thirty-five years ago by the dean of U.S. Catholic historians, John Tracy Ellis. At the May 1955 meeting of the Catholic Commission on Intellectual and Cultural Affairs, Ellis attempted to explain a criticism of American Catholicism first raised by the English scholar Denis Brogan, who had argued: "In no modern Western society is the intellectual prestige of Catholicism lower than in the country where, in such respects as wealth, numbers, and strength of organization, it is so powerful." Father Ellis believed that "no well-informed American Catholic [would] challenge that statement"; what interested him was how this sorry state of affairs had come to be.

Ellis suggested nine causal factors: (1) The abiding effects of the anti-Catholic prejudice that had been implanted in the English colonies in the seventeenth century. (2) The historical preoccupation of the American Church with the assimilation of huge numbers of immigrants. (3) The generally "non-intellectual, if not anti-intellectual, atmosphere in the United States." (4) The absence, despite the urgings of leaders like Bishop John Lancaster Spalding, of a distinctively Catholic intellectual tradition in America. (5) American Catholicism's "unchallenged acceptance" of the national tendency "to follow walks of life which promise high remuneration in terms of money." (6) The failure of clerical and lay Catholic leaders to appreciate the "vocation of the intellectual." (7) The failure of Catholic institutions of higher education to concentrate their efforts on fields "where Catholic thought counts most . . . *viz.* the humanities and the liberal arts." (8) The absence of a "love of scholarship for its own sake," even among Catholic educators. (9) The "pervading spirit of separatism" and "inferiority complex" that had long characterized American Catholicism.[21]

The ensuing debate over these claims,[22] and the question whether

Ellis's rather draconian judgment had a sustainable empirical basis,[23] need not detain us here, but we can pause to note several points. Ellis and those who supported him believed, first, that there was such a thing as a distinctively *Catholic* intellectual life; second, that there was no fundamental incompatibility between a classically Catholic intellectual world-view and American culture (the ongoing nativist problem notwithstanding); and third, that Catholic intellectuals ought to seek a distinctive "market share," based on a historic intellectual "comparative advantage," in the humanities and liberal arts, i.e., in the chief culture-forming disciplines of the academy. One can even sense, in Ellis's argument, a premonition of John Courtney Murray's later claim that in the construction of an American public philosophy of democratic pluralism, there was no richer intellectual resource to be tapped than classic Catholic understandings of the human person, human society, human history, and human destiny.[24] The problem was not "the Catholic tradition"; the problem was the insufficient vigor with which Catholic intellectuals were engaging that tradition in the ongoing tasks of democratic culture-formation.

The Too Easy Coherence of Integralism

By "the tradition," of course, what was usually meant in the Catholic 1950s was what Philip Gleason has called the "neo-Scholastic version of faith," in which "Catholicism came to be viewed as a culture, a total way of life. There was a 'Catholic viewpoint' on everything, a Catholic way of doing everything, even, I remember hearing, of tying one's shoes—but that was perhaps facetious."[25]

No doubt there was a much to be criticized in the more popularized forms of this distinctively Catholic integralism. It was unecumenical, indeed at times quite anti-ecumenical, and in its popular expressions it was too often sustained—psychologically and existentially, as well as theoretically—by a triumphalistically separatist ecclesiology. It tended to view education as indoctrination. And while it is true that during the 1950s such giants as Jacques Maritain were trying to engage neo-Scholasticism in dialogue with modern critical philosophy, few scholars in American Catholic institutions of higher education were paying much attention to the Frenchman's labors. 1950s Catholic integralism was also tempted to be ahistorical, particularly in its tendency to fix on one period of Church history—from the pontificate of Pius IX through that of Pius XII —as definitive of Catholic self-understanding.[26]

On the other hand, and there is always an "other hand," we should not too easily dismiss what Ellis, Murray, and Gleason thought was possible in the encounter between a refined and sharpened "integral" Catholicism and American culture, particularly when we look at what happened next: which was that "the problem" came to be identified, not with a rich tradition inadequately explored and extended, but with the tradition itself—with what Daniel Callahan dismissively called "the American Catholic mentality." Philip Gleason's summary of the post–Ellis/Murray turn-of-the-wheel is worth citing at length:

> While concepts like intellectualism and anti-intellectualism remained nebulous, a significant development took place between the mid-1950s and the mid-1960s. At first, most writers accepted the premise that although Catholics had made a poor showing as scholars and scientists they could do better simply by trying harder; no inherent incompatibility was posited between being Catholic and being an intellectual. As the controversy waxed, however, more and more Catholic attitudes and patterns of life and thought were listed as obstacles to intellectualism. In order to make a real intellectual breakthrough, it appeared that many things traditionally associated with Catholicism would have to be eliminated.
>
> This trend culminated in the affirmation that prior commitment to a dogmatic religious position could not be reconciled with "love of intellectuality for its own sake." In other words, true intellectualism was defined in such a way as to exclude religious commitment. To operate as an intellectual, the Catholic would have to set aside doctrinal beliefs. The notion that a person might legitimately employ his intellect —as an intellectual—to explicate or defend the Church's position was rejected by Edward Wakin and Joseph F. Scheuer in their book dealing with the "de-Romanization" of American Catholicism. The expression "intellectual apostolate," they wrote, is "a contradiction in terms"; the exhortation to Catholics to take it up "threatens to subvert the

intellectual and turn him into a holy panderer for the Catholic Church."

What happened, in short, was that a campaign which was intended to increase the number of Catholic intellectuals had reached the point of denying that there could be such a thing as a Catholic intellectual.[27]

In sum, and according to Philip Gleason, the baby was jettisoned along with the *intégriste* bathwater.

Now one could argue that the neo-Scholastic crust had become so thick that breaking through it, in order to "open the windows of the Church to the modern world" and bring about the *aggiornamento* of Vatican II, required not a chisel but a sledgehammer, with the attendant risk of shattering the whole structure. One could argue that. But it seems implausible. For at least one expression of the "integral" Catholicism of the 1950s appealed to some very bright people. Hard as it may be to remember today, the Catholic approach to scholarship that stressed the organic integration of the intellectual life, and the "relevance" (to use an unfortunately vulgarized word) of that integrative vision to the evolution of human culture and the right-ordering of human society—this approach found favor, not simply with committed Catholics such as Maritain, Gilson, and Murray,[28] but also with certifiable "Big Intellectuals" outside the family like Mortimer Adler, Robert Hutchins, Stringfellow Barr, and Mark Van Doren.

One could go even further and argue that the Ellis critique, contrary to its author's intentions, helped open the path to the abandonment (i.e., the view of Catholic intellectual life as "holy pandering") mourned by Gleason. In other words, one could argue that some American Catholic intellectuals in the immediate post-Conciliar generation internalized an image of pre-Conciliar Catholic intellectual life as irredeemably hidebound, ahistorical, and, in brief, out of it. Even the work of men such as Maritain and Murray, rather than being seen as a platform for development (and development was surely needed), would be dismissed as hopelessly *passé* or, more recently, in the case of Murray (once it had become important to "reclaim" him), proposed as a prolegomenon to the deconstructionist enterprise.[29]

Contemporary "restorationist" fantasies notwithstanding, post-Conciliar American Catholic intellectual life has not been character-ized *per essentiam* by a radical rejection of the past and a deconstruc-tive approach to the present and future. Among others, Avery Dulles, S.J., has shown that it is quite possible to be both attentive to the "Catholic classics" and committed to an exploration of what Murray would have called the "growing end" of the tradition. But other prominent American Catholic intellectuals have succumbed to the post-Ellis temptations suggested above.

Deconstructing the Pope

There is some irony in the fact that the thought and ministry of Pope John Paul II—a pope who is himself a practicing "intellec-tual"—have become a focal point for the polemics of these decon-structionists. Rosemary Radford Ruether writes of the Pope's sexist "pathology," which reinforces ecclesiastical "misogynists" who deny women "reproductive self-determination" (Professor Ruether means "abortion") in order to assuage "the need of the celibate male to punish women for their sexuality."[30]

One thinks also in this regard of Father Richard McBrien's relentless *bellum contra Wojtyla*. McBrien argues that, unlike Paul VI (who "urged compassion"), John Paul II is "tough-minded" (i.e., lacking compassion). Unlike the historically oriented thinking of Paul VI, John Paul II's intellect is "ahistorical." Paul's theology was "incarnational," while John Paul II's is "otherworldly." Paul VI "affirmed the world," while John Paul II "condemns it." All of which, *pace* McBrien, has to do with this pope's lamentable biogra-phy: "Karol Wojtyla has known only two kinds of political regimes in his adult life: Nazism and Communism," some of whose unsa-vory tactics he has learned only too well: "Brook no dissent, place hard-liners in positions of enforcement, make an example of those who deviate from the party line by punishment that is swift, firm and highly visible."[31]

Thus the view from the chairman's desk at the department of theology under the Golden Dome: John Paul II as totalitarian commissar. Karol Wojtyla's philosophical and theological work is surely not beyond the boundaries of reasonable argument. What

McBrien offers, however, is not analysis but a caricature, one that would be laughable if it weren't so wrongheaded.[32] And the problem that McBrien's and Ruether's "analyses" present is one not for John Paul II but for American Catholic intellectual life. For if these intellectual leaders cannot see in this pope one model of their own vocation—which is to be modern intellectuals without becoming uncritical modernists—then perhaps it is time for some latter-day John Tracy Ellis to lament, again, the sad state of American Catholic intellectual life: its aridity, its unreflective absorption of tradition (in this case, the "traditions"—and fads—of the American "new class"), its lack of *élan*, its boring dullness and smug predictability.

I don't think that time has yet arrived. But there are sufficient danger signals abroad in the land that Catholic intellectuals ought to ponder what Jewish humorists have called the classic Jewish telegram: "Start worrying. Letter follows."

THEMES FOR A REFORMATION

Neither the deconstructionist nor the restorationist impulse holds out much hope for the reformation and renaissance of American Catholic intellectual life that our community's numbers and resources (particularly in light of the "circulation of elites" in American religion identified by Roof and McKinney) make possible. The intellectual deficiencies of both of these enterprises are increasingly evident. Perhaps even more to the point, neither can be considered the "growing end" (as Murray would have put it) of American Catholic intellectual life. For one senses, in important sectors of that intellectual community, an intuition that the task before us is precisely the one identified by the Council, viz., a *dialogue* with modernity, rather than a monologue (the deconstructionist option) or a retreat into a mythical past (the restorationist proposal).

The following are four possible themes for jump-starting that two-way conversation.

1. We require a new reading of the contemporary American cultural situation, ahead of the standard left/right barricades, which, on closer examination, show a striking similarity.

There is a curious point of agreement between the deconstructionist and restorationist camps in their common judgment that

American culture is, well, just about appalling—fissiparously indi-
vidualistic, greedy, obsessed with material consumption, arrogant,
selfish. On this question, at least, the two ends of what is usually
presented as a spectrum of opinion meet, and the "spectrum"
reveals itself to be in fact a circle, or, to borrow from Chesterton, a
"narrow infinity."

Self-criticism is a staple feature of American culture and perhaps
reveals the ongoing influence of the Puritan ethic; as one friend
puts it, "there's no point in being American if you don't feel
guilty." But the facile resort to the cultural jeremiad often reveals,
not a rigorously critical (and self-critical) spirit, but a sloppy
acquiescence to one or another ideological orthodoxy, of the left
or of the right. The kind of American Catholic intellectual life that
can truly engage a dialogue with modernity would be getting
"ahead of the barricades" here to grapple vigorously with a number
of contemporary cultural analyses that stand the usual arguments
on their heads.

It would grapple, for example, with Jeffrey Stout's recent argument that public moral discourse in America is not in quite so
awful a shape as the early Alasdair MacIntyre,[33] and Robert Bellah
and his colleagues,[34] have thought, but is in fact open to what Stout
terms "Augustinian liberalism." This approach would mediate between the Enlightenment project (with its emphasis on the autonomous, individual moral agent) and the new community-based
"narrative ethics" of, *inter alia*, Stanley Hauerwas.[35] In doing so,
the new liberalism would reappropriate elements of the classic
Thomistic moral tradition, in conversation with what we might call
the neo–neo-Thomistic proposals made by the later MacIntyre in
Whose Justice? Which Rationality?[36]

The kind of Catholic intellectual life capable of a genuine dialogue with modernity would seriously engage, rather than derisively
dismiss (as happens from both left and right, from deconstructionists and restorationists), Michael Novak's analysis of the American
"communitarian individual," and Novak's related proposals for a
fresh conversation, informed by the American Catholic experience,
on the Church's traditional nervousness about the intellectual un-
derpinnings of liberal political and economic institutions.[37] (Such a
conversation would also be useful in engaging those arguments

from the Vatican that seem to assume a one-to-one correspondence between Western European secularization and contemporary American culture, and that tend to read the history of the modern quest for freedom exclusively through the lens of 1789, rather than through the quite different lens of 1776/1787.)

It would seek an ongoing conversation with the younger "communitarian liberals," like Harvard's Michael Sandel, in their efforts to define American public life as something other than life in a "republic of procedures" in which "rights" are reduced to juridical "trumps."[38] Concurrently, it would engage (rather than ignore or mock) the critique of post-war liberalism mounted by such Ur-conservatives as Russell Kirk.[39]

It would engage the new historiography of the American Founding adumbrated by William Lee Miller, who emphasizes that the Founders and Framers (and particularly Madison), far from being radical individualists, expected Americans to live in "a way whose hallmarks were . . . public virtue, public liberty, [the] public happiness of republicanism, the humane sociability of the Scottish Enlightenment."[40]

It would, in short, engage itself in a critique of American culture that pushed the argument ahead, rather than derivatively reflecting the widespread tendency (by no means limited to the fever swamps of the Left) to blame America first—and early. It would say of America, in the wonderful formulation of William Lee Miller, "Of thee, nevertheless, I sing."

2. We require a new (in fact, not-so-new) reading of the intentions of Vatican II.

It is a sad fact of the contemporary American Catholic intellectual scene that one risks embarrassment (at best) by citing the work of Joseph Ratzinger, or even works on the work of Joseph Ratzinger. But since the hermeneutics of Vatican II continue to play a central role in defining "Catholic intellectual life today," I would nonetheless make bold to suggest that Aidan Nichols's summary of the Council's intention—which concludes his study of Ratzinger's theological development and reflects his understanding of Ratzinger's approach to the interpretation of Vatican II—is well worth pondering:

The major constructive achievement of the Council was the recovery of the tradition of the pre-Tridentine Church, and notably of tradition in its crucial patristic phase when the Christian religion took on its classic form. It was a Council of patristic (and biblical) *ressourcement*, intended to usher Catholics into a larger room than that of the last few centuries. Moreover, the same theologians who forged this neo-patristic synthesis—essentially, the French and German language divines of the inter-war period—were convinced that it would provide a new basis on which to address the world of today and its problems. Its greater anthropological depth would enable the Church to be more human without becoming less divine.

Wholly admirable in itself, this programme turned out to have two flaws. First, though the Conciliar majority rightly perceived that "traditional Catholicism" of the kind now represented by Archbishop Marcel Lefebvre and his followers was really little more ancient than their grandmothers, they underestimated the disorienting effect of its supplanting. In depriving Catholics of the language in which they had habitually ordered their religious universe and through which they had come to their own self-understanding, the displacement of the immediately pre-Conciliar tradition, essentially the product of the sixteenth-century Catholic Reformation and the Catholic revival of the nineteenth century, generated a sense of *anomie*, an obscuring of corporate and personal identity. . . .

Secondly, the unity of the Council's twin imperatives of *ressourcement* and *aggiornamento*, founded as this was on the theological anthropology of the Fathers, proved more fragile than had been expected. Once *aggiornamento* had parted company from *ressourcement*, adaptation could degenerate into mere accommodation to habits of mind and behavior in secular culture. Using the excuse of pastoral necessity, *insouciance* towards the tradition as a whole might be justified or even obligatory in an effort to relate the hypothetically reconstructed Christian origin to contemporary needs and expectations. Many of those needs and expectations must, indeed, be taken with great seriousness. However, the manner in which the Christian origin ("the Gospel") is related ("relevant") to them cannot be determined by overshooting the past: that is what "Tradition" means. The task today is to take forward the constructive moment of the Council's achievement: the binding of tradition and contemporaneity into a living unity.[41]

A balanced judgment on contemporary American Catholic intellectual life would concede that, our notable accomplishments notwithstanding, we have in general done a very poor job of presenting the Council as an enterprise based on the "twin imperatives of *ressourcement* and *aggiornamento*." Indeed, the notion of Vatican II as a council of *ressourcement* is primarily notable for its absence from our discourse.

This has fed both the deconstructionist and the restorationist impulse, in different ways. The deconstructionist failure may be taken, in symbolic terms, as a failure to heed the words of Jesus to his disciples at the multiplication of loaves and fishes: "Gather up the fragments left over, that nothing may be lost" (John 6:12). Works such as *The Church in Anguish: Has the Vatican Betrayed Vatican II?* (see note 30) leave the impression that "the fragments" are indeed so much detritus to be left behind, and good riddance. Conversely, the restorationists' failure to link a true patristic *ressourcement* to *aggiornamento* has led to an identification of "the sources," not with Origen and Cyril and Gregory Nazianzen and Basil and Augustine, but with the theological manuals of the 1950s. In neither case has the question for American Catholics become, "How much of this rich and ancient and growing tradition can I make my own?" Rather, the debased question has become, on the left, "How little can I still believe and be a Catholic?," and on the right, "How can we get those liberal characters out of the family?"

Intellectuals usually take too much credit for some things, and are too often prematurely blamed for others, but in this instance I think consciences have to be examined. Have we adequately engaged the Council as a council of *both ressourcement* and *aggiornamento*? Or have we been too busy politicking (within and without the Church) to pay much attention to the problem, even when we are confronted by the pathetic ignorance of their tradition that marks so many Catholic undergraduates and seminarians?

3. We require a new vision of the "authoritative," one that goes beyond the sterile alternatives of "authoritarianism" and the pursuit of the "autonomous" self.

The language is that of Richard John Neuhaus,[42] in proposing that ours is a "Catholic moment" in American history:

In our individual lives, the trajectory of growth is from authoritarianism, through autonomy, to an acknowledgment of what is authoritative. As in individual life, so this trajectory is also evident in the lives of institutions and communities. As a general proposition, authoritarianism may be viewed as the premodern, autonomy as the modern, and acknowledgment of the authoritative as the postmodern modes of existence. . . . Vatican II offered relief from what was widely perceieved to be an authoritarian church structure. There followed a period of heady freedom, of release from boundaries. This was the phase of autonomy, and almost nobody denies that it gave rise to many excesses, some of which may have been dangerous, many of which were just silly. Silly and yet understandable, for the excesses of the release were in direct proportion to the excesses of the prior oppression—or at least what some people thought to be the prior oppression.

Much of contemporary Catholicism is still in the autonomy phase.[43]

Including, I would argue, much of American Catholic intellectual life. We are still desperately battling over issues of "church authority." Many of those issues are of great importance. But an obsession with them may keep us from paying sufficient attention to the far more important question, "What is authoritative for the Church?"

This question now being pressed in an impressively ecumenical fashion by men such as George Lindbeck, Thomas Oden, Thomas Hopko, and William Lazareth (from the worlds of mainline Protestantism, Orthodoxy, and Lutheranism), as well as by a host of younger evangelical Protestant scholars.[44] I welcome this new Protestant and Orthodox scholarship. But I hope it will be complemented by many more Catholic contributions to the definition of the evangelically and ecclesially authoritative than are evident today.[45]

4. We require a different vision of the "public Church" when Roman Catholicism in America turns its attention to issues of domestic and international policy.

Although this is my special interest, I have left the "politics" to the end. The reason is that I have become convinced that the kind of "public Church" capable of taking leadership in the reconstruction of American public philosophy, and capable of being a distinctively ecclesial participant in and critic of the public policy arena, will not emerge until the issues identified above are, at the very least, raised and debated intelligently. Assuming, perhaps optimistically, that that debate gets under way, then what? What kind of "public Church" would we be?

As far as boundary-setting goes, we would not be a church that thought forming the consciences of individual Catholics exhausted its public responsibilities. Nor would the "prophetic witness" model as usually understood in the American Catholic new class define our role. Still less would the Church be widely perceived as a faction in a partisan camp on questions of domestic and foreign policy.[46]

As for the alternative, ahead of today's barricades, the "public Church" capable of seizing the Catholic moment would take as its first responsibility the re-creation of a civil public square in which genuine moral argument about the right-ordering of the American experiment can take place. To put it another way, Catholic intellectuals and bishops ought to help create the circumstances in which the Church's voice can indeed be heard as the voice of a publicly welcome and publicly effective pastor and teacher.[47]

That is not the "public Church" we have today, which in its post-Conciliar entry into the public policy lists has become widely and accurately identified as the bearer of a partisan agenda. Some of its stands on public policy I agree with; on others I disagree (no surprise, that!). But my primary concern is not the correspondence (or lack thereof) between my own policy positions and those of the United States Catholic Conference, for these are matters of "prudential judgment" about which reasonable folk can and do disagree. My real worry is far more fundamental: that we are missing a historic opportunity to address, if not complete, the "Murray Project"—the construction of an American public philosophy capable of sustaining disciplined (if occasionally raucous) public moral argument about the ordering of our lives, loves, and loyalties in this republic. This has to be the first order of business. Unless it is at least begun, the conditions for the possibility of a morally informed policy debate will not exist.

To argue for this redefinition of priorities in the "public Church" is not to be anti-ecumenical, for the creation of a religiously informed "public philosophy" is assuredly an ecumenical task in the United States. Nor is it to propose a retreat from the public square, which after all encompasses far more than the institutions found at either end of Pennsylvania Avenue. But it is to recognize that classic Catholic political theory, with its roots in the natural-law ethic, is a precious resource for the Church's fundamental task, *as Church*, in our public life. That task is not a simple matter of voting yea or nay on this or that. Rather, it involves nurturing the many public arenas (not all of them governmental by any means) in which the ongoing renewal of the American experiment is debated. The possibility of a distinctive Catholic contribution to this fundamental public business is increasingly recognized by ecumenically oriented public theologians; it is time to explore more adequately the treasures buried beneath our own feet.[48]

The Enlarged Conversation

How would these themes, pursued, effect a reformation in American Catholic intellectual life? Most simply, but perhaps most importantly, they would create a wider historical conversation by relativizing and debunking the ideology of modernity. In other words, they would open us again to the full range of Christian wisdom, key elements of which have gotten lost in the race to appear thoroughly *au courant* according to the standards of the contemporary American academy.

In addition to reintroducing us to what Father George Florovsky called the "ecumenism of time," the themes I am suggesting here would also, if carefully probed, drive us back toward that classic Catholic "scandal of particularity," in terms of both the foundational scandal of Christian faith (Galatians 5:11), the incarnation of God in Jesus of Nazareth, and the particular American experience of that revelation of God in Christ. Reclaiming that dimension of the Catholic tradition would, in turn, make us better prepared to combat those gnostic currents in modern consciousness that are a fundamental challenge to the enfleshed revelation that is the *sine qua non* of Christian faith and the community to which it gives birth.

This task of reclamation and extension is, happily, one to which self-critical thinkers more usually attuned to either the deconstructionist or the restorationist enterprise seem increasingly open. Perhaps, in the history of ideas (and of intellectuals), it was inevitable that the ideologization of modernity and of the critical method would itself come under critique: just as it could be expected that people who use fax machines would eventually see some incongruity between that experience and a definition of "orthodoxy" that is pre-modern and ahistorical. However one sorts out those probabilities, though, a new openness—a post-modern openness, if you will—is discernible in various quarters of American Catholic intellectual life. And God be thanked, say I.

CONVERSATIONS ON THE FAR SIDE OF COMPLEXITY

The term "post-modern" is deployed to identify an astonishing range of phenomena, from Philip Johnson's design of the AT&T headquarters in New York to the theological speculations of George Lindbeck. Yet for all its ubiquity (and consequent flaccidness), "post-modern" remains a useful designator of the kind of American Catholic intellectual life I think is aborning—none too soon.

By "post-modern American Catholic intellectual life," I mean a multi-disciplinary community of conversation that: recognizes that the Enlightenment project, with its emphasis on the autonomous person (and autonomous reason, and autonomous conscience, and so forth) has run its course; recognizes that there are things to be learned from that project, but candidly admits that it in no sense constitutes the Everest of human intellectual and moral endeavor; and wishes to devise fresh approaches to the age-old problem of Catholicism and culture in an environment that is neither nostalgically pre-modern (*pace* the restorationists) nor compulsively modern (*pace* the deconstructionists) but distinctively post-modern, with emphasis on both adverb and adjective.

Neither the restorationist nor the deconstructionist approach to the perennial question of Catholicism and culture will do. Both reflect the unsatisfactory "Christ *of* culture" paradigm analyzed in H. Richard Niebuhr's classic, *Christ and Culture*.[49] In that model, the Church takes its culture-forming cues, not from the complex richness of its own variegated tradition (itself formed, of course, in dialectical interaction with different cultures), but from a narrow and historically contingent set of social, political, and cultural arrangements. This is what both deconstructionists and restorationists do: the former as a chaplaincy to the American new class, and the latter in its efforts to "fix" the final expression of Catholic orthodoxy in, say, 1952.

The Contours of Post-Modernity

The American Catholic intellectual life I hope to see unfold in this closing decade of the second millennium is one that, to borrow from Paul Ricoeur and Alfred North Whitehead, explores that "second naïveté" which lies, not in pre-modern simplicities or modern complexifications, but "on the far side of complexity." Such an intellectual life would be one that has indeed, to try another metaphor, passed through the "fiery brook" (of Feuerbach), but has also truly *passed through* that great divide between moderns (and post-moderns) and pre-moderns. Unlike the restorationists, it would have taken the plunge, so to speak; but unlike the deconstructionists, it would not be treading water halfway across.

To put it yet another way, this intellectual life will have experienced relativity—that most distinctive of "modern" intellectual traits—without becoming relativistic. Brigitte and Peter Berger have captured this attitude in the following terms:

> The experience of relativity was classically formulated by Pascal in his statement that what is truth on one side of the Pyrenees is error on the other. It cannot be stated emphatically enough [and this *contra* the deconstructionist impulse] that this does *not* imply that there is no such thing as truth; it hardly needs saying that Pascal, of all people, intended no such implication. The experience of relativity, however, makes it difficult to hold beliefs in the taken-for-granted, untroubled way that has always been characteristic of tradition [I would say "of restorationists"]. The individual who has passed through the experience may hold very firm beliefs, but he will be conscious of the fact that he has *chosen* them. The traditionalist [restorationist] holds his beliefs as giv-

ens. Modernization, at its very core, is a movement of the mind from destiny to choice.

To be modern, however critically, means to assent to this movement. . . . To the traditionalist, all this theorizing is part and parcel of the intellectual degeneration of modernity, the alleged diagnosis that is in fact the disease.[50]

If to be "modern" means to enter into the experience of relativity, to be "post-modern," as I use the term, means to relativize the relativizers, to reject relativism, and to press ahead toward a creative identification of, and intellectual engagement with, the truly authoritative. In the theological community this will involve, to repeat, both *ressourcement* and *aggiornamento*.

It will involve, for all of us, the development of a post-modern but classically grounded sense of Catholicism's unitive vision. The "Catholic sensibility," writes John Breslin, S.J., is one that rejects a pendular view of "the Church's progress through time" in favor of a kind of evolutionary spiral: "Circularity, yes, but not simple repetition. With each turn of the spiral we move upward even as we swing back over our past, for the Resurrection of Jesus sprang us out of our two-dimensional prison into a universe with a divinely stamped future."[51]

To be sure, this image can, absent due cautions (particularly in terms of one's view of progress in history), decay into a form of happy-talk Teilhardianism, whose contemporary American analogues may be found in "New Age" currents of thought. But Breslin rightly reminds us that classic Catholicism has within it "an attitude that avoids . . . extremes, instinctively preferring the conjunctive 'and' to the disjunctive 'or.' "[52] This was the attitude of Thomas Aquinas, in his own day a kind of post-modern. This was the attitude of John Carroll, James Gibbons, and John Courtney Murray toward the question of Catholicism and the American democratic experiment. It is an attitude that ought to inform our efforts to sketch the contours of a post-modern American Catholic intellectual life today.

The Necessity of Persuasion

Those efforts will be frustrated if they are not shaped by a sense of proportion, a sense of humility, and a sense of hope. David

Tracy has written about the evangelical necessity of persuasion, as distinguished from coercion, in Catholic intellectual life:

> When persuasion is abandoned, the vacuum is soon filled by the furies let loose by coercion. Along that way lies presumption for the few and despair for the many. But presumption and despair are theological vices whose only service is to clarify anew the need for hope as the central theological virtue of our period—a hope grounded in faith, intellectual integrity, and courage; a hope functioning as the love empowering all true persuasion in the community of hope.[53]

Who could disagree? But perhaps Father Tracy will allow me this gloss on his call to hope and persuasion: The forces of coercion in American Catholic intellectual life today cannot be identified solely (I would say, primarily) with the institutional locales that once brought us the Americanist controversy and *Testem Benevolentiae*, and their putative contemporary American organizational allies. Indeed, I would argue, in all charity, that the post-Conciliar American Catholic intellectual establishment's quest for power has been successful far beyond the most fevered nightmares of Catholics United For the Faith. To put it another way, the call to persuasion we need today, if it is to be at the service of the whole Church, ought to be addressed in the first instance to the leadership and followership in our own American Catholic intellectual community. That being done, our ongoing conversation with those resident on the Piazza del Santo Uffizio might be far more fruitful.

Finally, the quest for a post-modern American Catholic intellectual life requires a deepened sense of the intellectual vocation as an *ecclesial* calling. Hundreds of articles have been written since the Council under the title "Why I Stay in the Church," or somesuch. Karl Rahner found this an "abominable" way to frame the question:

> Faith can be attacked; I can also imagine someone losing this ecclesial dimension of faith without feeling any guilt before God. But the real Christian believer can't possibly have a patronizing attitude toward the Church that allows him or her to weigh staying in the Church against getting out of it. Relationship to the Church is at the very essence, an absolute of Christian faith. And one should be able to detect this when people who claim to

be people of the Church, members of the Church, criticize their Church. Those who stand outside the Church or for whom the Church is not an integral part of faith but only an enormous sociological accident which they have entered by chance, may judge the Church differently. One should be able to tell from the criticism whether it is formulated by someone who does or does not have a real relationship to the Church. . . . When criticism flows from the center of the Church's common life, it is justified, even a necessary and sacred responsibility. But only then. We should leave criticisms of another kind to those who have rejected the Church. We should not flatter them.[54]

This—from the perspective of a German Jesuit, a transcendental Thomist and professional theologian—strikes me as not all that different from the perspective on faith, culture, and the life of the mind with which we began: that of a single Southern woman whose craft was fiction. Flannery O'Connor was hardly a Rahnerian.[55] But that doesn't matter. The point of contact between these two great spirits—the point on which American Catholic intellectuals need to reflect, these days—is the experience and vocation of being intellectually alive *in the Church*, where, we are taught by Irenaeus of Lyons, we find the glory of God that is man fully alive in Christ.

Witness to that saving reality is our basic task, whatever our disciplinary specialties. Fidelity to that vocation is, if I understand the tradition, the measure by which Catholic intellectuals will be judged. On this, I think, there is considerable agreement. And that is ground for hope, and a measure of good cheer.

6

Capturing the Story Line: The New Historiography of American Catholicism

Catholics in America have rarely taken the study of their history seriously. My own circumstances, which were hardly unique, may illustrate the point: in nineteen years (1956–75) of a generally excellent Catholic education in church-sponsored schools and seminaries, I never once was offered a formal course in the history of Catholicism in the United States. And while this educational gap was perhaps understandable in a church dominated by immigrants and their children until the very recent past, it is nonetheless a formidable problem today, for "not to know what happened before one was born is always to be a child." Or so Cicero (*De oratore*, II) thought.

Happily, there are signs, in the early 1990s, that this self-inflicted amnesia is ending. American Catholic history may not be so booming a discipline as biblical studies or "medical ethics," but even the most cursory survey of the *American Catholic Studies Newsletter* (published by the Cushwa Center for the study of American Catholicism at the University of Notre Dame, itself an institutional expression of the growth of the field) reveals an extraordinary range of research, ranging from classic institutional histories and biographies of key figures to the new social history with its emphases on patterns of community, spirituality, family life, and education. Many Catholic dioceses are, at long last, taking their archival responsibilities seriously, and new lodes of information are being unearthed and mined. For example, the Archdiocese

129

of Boston recently discovered and acquired twenty boxes of the personal and administrative papers of Cardinal Richard Cushing, once thought to have been destroyed at the cardinal's death in 1970.[1]

This new vitality of interest in the American Catholic story is surely to the good: it is good for the Church (both here and in Rome), good for the study of American religion, and good for a more comprehensive understanding of the complex interaction of religion and public life in the ongoing experiment that is American democracy. But there are no unmixed blessings in the tides of intellectual interest and fashion, as the discovery of Clio's charism among American Catholics illustrates. For parallel to (and in some cases generating) the explosion of historical knowledge about American Catholicism has come an effort to put that knowledge— better, a distinctive interpretation of that knowledge—to various partisan purposes in today's struggles over the meaning of ortho-doxy, authority, and ministry. Separating the wheat from that particular form of chaff is the business of this essay.

THE CLASSIC STORY LINE

To say that American Catholics have rarely taken their history seriously is not to say that there have never been serious historians of American Catholicism. Although they are largely unknown outside the American Catholic community (and scarcely better known inside it, for that matter), John Gilmary Shea, Peter Guilday, and, preeminently, John Tracy Ellis were old-fashioned historians of genuine accomplishment who, in the late nineteenth century and the first half of the twentieth, created the classic story line of American Catholicism.

It was a story written under the long shadow of nativist (and, it must be said, largely Protestant) anti-"Romanism" and its recurring charge that Catholicism—as a body of doctrine, a matter of per-sonal conviction, and an institution—was incompatible with Amer-ican democratic republicanism.[2] Msgr. Ellis has frequently quoted the remark made to him by Professor Arthur Schlesinger, Sr., that Schlesinger considered "the prejudice against your Church as the deepest bias in the history of the American people."[3] There is ample evidence even today to suggest, without getting into a bigotry sweepstakes, that Professor Schlesinger's indictment was not a reckless one.[4]

Classic American Catholic historians, as eager to challenge the nativist canard as other pre-Conciliar Catholic intellectuals, adopted the "Catholicism/Americanism" tension as the principal theme of their story line. They sought to show how the Catholic people, and particularly their episcopal leaders, had worked tirelessly to demonstrate in practice what they affirmed in principle: that there was no inherent conflict in being both a convinced Catholic and a patriotic American. Thus historical classicists like Shea, Guilday, and Ellis tended to highlight those great accomplishments of the Church in the United States—the assimilation of some ten million immigrants between the early nineteenth and early twentieth centuries, and the massive institution-building that paralleled the assimilation—that graphically and empirically refuted the spirit (and the letter) of Know-Nothingism. The brick-and-mortar church of the urban neighborhoods thus became the main character in the American Catholic story.

Given their (wholly justifiable) concerns over problems of religious intolerance, the classic historians of American Catholicism, after a few ritual nods toward the Church of the Spanish and French explorers, liked to begin The Story of American Catholicism in 1634, with the founding of the proprietary colony of Maryland as, *inter alia*, a refuge for Catholics from Stuart England. These historians paid particular attention to the Maryland Act of Religious Toleration, which in 1649 provided that no Christian in the province would "bee any wais troubled, molested or discountenanced for or in respect of his or her religion nor in the free exercise thereof," nor could any person be in "any way compelled to the beleife or exercise of any Religion against his or her consent."[5]

The "Carroll Church"

The story was then fast-forwarded to the time of the American Revolution. The 35,000 Catholics in the thirteen colonies were less than one per cent of the national population. But they were nonetheless blessed by great leaders, most prominent among them the Carroll cousins, Charles Carroll of Carrollton (last surviving signer of the Declaration of Independence) and John Carroll, first archbishop of Baltimore and the first Catholic bishop in the United States. The "Carroll Church" was, in fact, the paradigm of American Catholicism most celebrated by the classic historians, and John Carroll himself was invariably presented as a model of leadership that his successors in the American episcopate would do well to emulate.

Archbishop Carroll's patriotism and his optimism about the American experiment; his ecumenism and his commitment to the constitutional separation of church and state; his active role in civic life; his passion for Catholic education; his non-sycophantic loyalty to the Holy See—these qualities of the "Maryland Tradition" were regularly celebrated in the classic historiography of American Catholicism, for it was precisely these qualities that, according to the standard account, allowed American Catholicism to weather the nativist assault and to get on with the parallel tasks of church-building and nation-building.[6] Great episcopal figures of the ante-bellum period—for example, the Irish liberal John England of Charleston, and the pugnacious John Hughes of New York—were "fitted" into the Carrollingian story line (if I may be pardoned the neologism) even as their distinctive styles and the accomplishments of their episcopates stretched the boundaries of the "Carroll Church." That style of Catholicism proved its tensile strength during the national cataclysm of 1861–65. Its unity in, and with, Rome kept American Catholicism from fracturing during the Civil War, according to the standard account. But the Church's (primarily Irish) ethnic concerns, and its nervousness about its position in the old Confederacy and the border states, conspired to keep it from seizing the great evangelical opportunity presented by black freedmen during Reconstruction.

The "Americanism" Controversy

The classic story line accelerated, and the central drama within it intensified, in the late nineteenth century. Here, the narrative was dominated by the struggle between the "Americanist" party (Cardinal James Gibbons of Baltimore, Archbishop John Ireland of St.

Paul, Bishop John Keane of Catholic University, and their Roman agent, Msgr. Denis O'Connell) on the one hand, and the "conservatives" (led by Archbishop Michael Corrigan of New York and his suffragan, the redoubtable Bernard McQuaid of Rochester) on the other—and it was rather clearly understood, in the classic story line, that the Americanists were, frankly, the good guys. Things were, of course, more complicated than that. Bishop McQuaid, the curmudgeonly "conservative," initially opposed the definition of papal infallibility at Vatican I.[7] Archbishop Ireland, the quintessential "liberal," ruthlessly drove Eastern-rite Catholic emigrants and their married clergy out of the archdiocese of St. Paul and indeed out of the Church (thus earning himself the ironic title, among some wags, of "father of Russian Orthodoxy in America").[8]

But where the two parties clearly divided was on the question of American democracy and its distinctive "answer" to the age-old problem of church and state. The Americanists supported, even celebrated, the American arrangement, while the conservatives (like most senior Roman officials of the day) found it tolerable at best. Charges of heresy flew back and forth.

Eventually, in 1899, the "Americanism" controversy was brought to a formal conclusion by Leo XIII's apostolic letter, *Testem Benevolentiae*. The letter condemned certain "Americanist" propositions (about spirituality, ecclesiology, the Church and modernity, and church/state relations); but the pope also admitted his uncertainty that anyone of consequence in the American Church held to the proscribed notions. In the ensuing hermeneutic battle, Gibbons and his party argued that "Americanism" was a "phantom heresy" (a position adopted by the classic historians of American Catholicism), while Corrigan and his friends thanked Rome for having saved them from the clutches of irresponsible Gallican innovators and sweaty jingoists.

The Carroll/Gibbons tradition, according to the classic story line, went into a fallow period after the deaths of the giants, Ireland in 1918 and Gibbons in 1921. The end game of the Americanist struggle abutted the far more stringent Roman reaction to "Modernism" in the first and second decades of the twentieth century, and the "Maryland Tradition" of Carroll and Gibbons was superceded by the vigorous *Romanitá* exemplified by Cardinal William O'Connell of Boston.[9] But the great tradition revived in the late 1940s and 1950s under the episcopal leadership of men like Detroit's Edward Mooney, Chicago's Albert Meyer, and St. Louis's Joseph Ritter, and reached a particularly sharp edge of intellectual development at the Jesuits' Woodstock College in rural Maryland, which housed the pioneer ecumenist Gustave Weigel and the great theologian of freedom, John Courtney Murray. The Second Vatican Council endorsed this revival, and indeed the tradition of the Carroll/Gibbons Church, in its "Declaration on Religious Freedom" (of which Murray was, of course, an intellectual architect).

By the mid-1960s, then, the tension that had driven the classic story line in the history of American Catholicism seemed largely resolved. The election of John F. Kennedy to the presidency in 1960, and the Vatican Council's endorsement of religious liberty as a fundamental human right, vindicated the confidence of Catholics in America and the American experience of Catholicism. Or so it seemed, until the ecclesiastical and political controversies of the post-Conciliar and Vietnam periods began to chip away at The Story of American Catholicism as told by the classicists.

THE STORY LINE REVISED

The classic story line held in the generation of scholars immediately following Msgr. Ellis. James Hennesey,[10] Gerald Fogarty,[11] and Marvin O'Connell[12] are three distinguished historians who, with differences of emphasis and nuance, have generally worked within the standard account while correcting its simplifications and amplifying its range of interests and concerns. Hennesey's 1981 volume *American Catholics* enriched the classic portrait of Catholic Americans by focusing on Catholicism as a community of distinctive human beings, and not simply as a religious institution. Fogarty's study *The Vatican and the American Hierarchy From 1870 to 1965* offered a detailed portrait of the (sometimes tawdry) ecclesiastical politics that shaped the Americanist controversy, but, again, from within the general framework of the standard account with its emphasis on the "normative" status of the Carroll/Gibbons view of the American Church.[13] In a more recent work, *American Catholic Biblical Scholarship: A History From the Early Republic to Vatican II,*[14]

Fogarty offers, among other things, a useful antidote to the claims of some Catholic "restorationists" that the anti-Modernist excesses of the early twentieth century were the invention of fevered post–Vatican II liberal imaginations; Fogarty's portrait of the persecution (there is no other word for it) of the Catholic University biblical scholar Henry Poels is a sobering reminder of how zeal for the Lord can, in the wrong hands, become mere zealotry. And Marvin O'Connell's recent, and splendid, study, *John Ireland and the American Catholic Church*, has demonstrated that biography in the grand manner, and within the classic story line, is still possible even as contemporary research refines the standard account and our understanding of the major figures within it.

But Fathers Hennesey, Fogarty, and O'Connell may well be a diminishing minority among current scholars of American Catholic history: for they seem to accept, with various qualifications, the Shea/Guilday/Ellis historiography in its general outline of The Story of American Catholicism. And it is precisely that account that is now being challenged by a revisionist school whose manifesto may be taken to be Jay P. Dolan's 1983 work *The American Catholic Experience*.[15]

The Revisionist Strategy

The revisionists have brought new insights into the study of American Catholic history, particularly in terms of social history. Like Fernand Braudel and the *Annalistes* school in France, and in a manner not dissimilar to that of E. P. Thompson, Eric Hobsbawm, and other Marxist historians in Britain, the revisionists are far less inclined, as a matter of principle, to investigate the doings of bishops and clergy, and far more interested in probing the daily lives and religious practices of American Catholics. This has, as I say, enriched our understanding of the American Catholic mosaic considerably.[16]

But the revisionists' real passion is historiographic. And their strategy, as an intellectual party, includes two lines of attack: to uproot the Shea/Guilday/Ellis standard account, and to replace it with a telling of the tale more congenial to their own current ecclesiastical concerns, which involve the catalogue of "progressive" causes flogged weekly in the *National Catholic Reporter*—disentangling the American Church from "Rome" (meaning, from the program of Pope John Paul II and Cardinal Joseph Ratzinger), "women's rights" in the Church, the "democratization" of Catholicism, and so forth.

If the classic story line stressed the essential continuity of the normative "Carroll Church" from the American Revolution to Vatican II (while taking account of the break in that trajectory occasioned by the Americanist and Modernist crises and the interwar "Romanization" of the American hierarchy), the revisionist story line stresses discontinuity: between the colonial period and the Church of the Revolutionary period; between the first, "republican" years of Carroll's episcopate and his later, "conservative" period; between the Carroll Church and the "immigrant Church" that followed; between, most importantly, the working-class "Catholic ghetto Church" of 1925–55 and the post-Conciliar suburban Church of the 1960s and 1970s.[17]

There was, to be sure, something a bit too neat about the standard account and its stress on continuity, particularly in the scholarly generations running from Shea through the early Ellis. Yet what the revisionists propose is not to refine that account but to abandon it. The story line they would substitute is one whose thematic hallmarks are: discontinuity across the generations from John Carroll to Joseph Bernardin and John O'Connor; the radical plurality of Catholic experience; the mediocrity and xenophobia of the pre-Conciliar ghetto Church; and a chronic, usually nasty, tension between the Church in America and the Holy See.

This revisionist strategy involves a root-and-branch retelling of the American Catholic story from its beginnings. In terms of the colonial period, the good news is that the new historians have probed far more deeply than their predecessors into the non-English-Catholic roots of Catholicism in America, and have added significantly to our store of knowledge about colonial French and Spanish Catholicism—the latter, of course, being of particular importance today given the prominent (and increasing) Hispanic presence in the American Church. The bad news is that the revisionists pay little attention to the Maryland colonial experience, and undervalue its importance as a breakthrough in religious tolerance with implications for Catholic participation in the subsequent church/state debate in the independent United States.

Indeed, the revisionist rereading of the Maryland colonial experience is a striking example of the school's tendency to turn what ought to be an amplification of our understanding of the past into an assault on the truth of the classic story line. The revisionists are surely right to remind us that the Calverts, founders of Maryland, were not plaster saints, but rather investors and proprietors who expected their colony to turn a profit. But why should such commercial concerns be thought to have precluded a commitment to religious liberty? Why couldn't the early Calverts have been *both* proprietors and exponents of religious tolerance? Is "progressive" American Catholicism's deprecation of "capitalism" lurking beneath the surface here and skewing the historiography?

John Carroll Under Assault

But the real target of the revisionist rereading of the American Catholic "founding" is the work and reputation of Archbishop John Carroll. In the recently published six-volume Bicentennial History of the Catholic Church in the United States,[18] James Hennesey sums up, in contemporary form and with due regard for the archbishop's flaws, the classic case for Carroll:

> His church was that which antedated in Catholicism the neo-ultramontane movement. In secular politics he was a Federalist, a conservative, an admirer of George Washington. The "furious democracy" of France's revolution appalled him. . . . But he did not confuse [the] American and French revolutions, and he believed that the church in the United States should be open to new forms of being and functioning that responded to the new setting in which it found itself. His working out of this in practice was not always easy nor was it always successful. John Carroll's "learning and abilities" were put fully to the test. On balance he met that test. His like has scarcely been known again in the history of American Catholicism.[19]

Jay P. Dolan, on the other hand, will have none of this. In *The American Catholic Experience*, Dolan's final judgment on John Carroll is little less than scathing, for Dolan regards Carroll as having committed a kind of treason: Carroll, who had the opportunity to lead the way, in fact betrayed the possibility of creating a distinctively "American Church" by his ultimate (and, in Dolan's view, pusillanimous) acquiescence to Roman authority.[20]

This view is, of course, dependent on Dolan's revisionist account of Carroll's early ministry as Superior of the Catholic Mission in the United States and as first bishop of Baltimore. Then, Dolan argues, Carroll understood the importance of creating a "republican" form of Catholicism in which the Church would absorb the new national experiment in democracy into its own internal life. Lay ownership and control of church properties, the election of bishops, decentralized church authority, a vernacular liturgy, eschewal of a distinct Catholic educational system—in short, Catholic Congregationalism: this was the cause that, Dolan believes, Carroll should have espoused and would have led, had he not been spooked, as it were, by the excesses of Jacobinism in France and his own innate ecclesiastical conservatism.

Those who detect some affinity between Professor Dolan's revisionist designs for the truly "republican" episcopate of John Carroll and the agenda of certain parties à gauche in American Catholicism today will not be far off the mark. For just as revisionist historiographers of the Cold War reread the history of the Truman administration through the steamy lens of their own Vietnam passions, the new American Catholic revisionists view the episcopate of John Carroll—the paradigm in the classic story line—through the prism of their own agenda for Catholicism in the 1990s. Thus Margaret Mary Reher, in an otherwise moderately positive assessment of Carroll in the Bicentennial History series, still feels compelled to complain that "John Carroll was comfortable when dealing with women in traditional roles of wife and mother or religious sister. When a woman crossed over the boundary into supposedly masculine territory, he had some reservations." Moreover, Carroll "betrayed an elitist strain in 1791, when he told one congregation composed of poor Irish and prominent French, that the 'best pew shall be reserved for the [French consul].' "[21] Minutiae, perhaps, but indicative of a cast of mind in which Archbishop Rembert Weakland—to adopt a symbolic reference point—stands in judgment on Archbishop John Carroll, and not the other way around.

In the Ghetto

Despite a flurry of "independent" thinking during the Americanist controversy, the "republican" Catholicism that Archbishop Carroll allegedly betrayed lay essentially dormant in American Catholicism until the post-Conciliar period, according to the revisionist story line. The 165 years between Carroll's "turning" and the close of the Second Vatican Council were dominated by the construction of the "immigrant Church"—by which the revisionists mean (sometimes making it explicit, and sometimes being a tad more subtle) the "ghetto Church." Moreover, "ghetto" here takes on the dreariest possible coloration: xenophobic, anti-intellectual, racist, sexist, authoritarian, Jansenist. Thomas Spalding, author of a new history of the archdiocese of Baltimore, sums up the revisionist indictment in these terms:

> In an editorial entitled "Keeping Up with the Times," the *Baltimore Catholic Review* told its readers in the summer of 1921 that the Church "sees beyond the present and prepares for other times when jazz and noise and vulgarity shall have sickened their votaries." Her attitude toward the big questions "is the same today as yesterday." As non-Catholic America entered a period of doubt and disillusionment following World War I, "Catholics set out as 'providential hosts' to defend the values and promises of American idealism which seemed threatened by various forms of irrationalism." In their keeping innocence would survive.
>
> With a self-assurance that brooked no questioning, American Catholics would convince themselves that they were in the forefront of every important social, cultural, and intellectual movement in the country. . . . Catholics would be daily reassured in the Catholic classroom, Catholic press, and Catholic pulpit that their Church had the answer to every question worth asking. Never would they think to look beyond these sources for confirmation.
>
> "We were, thus, a chosen people—though chosen, it seemed, to be second rate," recalled Garry Wills, a beneficiary of these reassurances and for several years a resident of Baltimore. The inbuilt inferiority of the ghetto church was carefully hidden by an apologetics ultimately rooted in neo-Thomism that would allow even literate Catholics to assume a God-given superiority. Upon

this apologetical undergirding the Catholic ghetto of the twenti-eth century would be confidently constructed.[22]

The classic story line, particularly in the hands of its more sophisticated practitioners, did not ignore the "immigrant Church"; indeed, it gave considerable attention to the assimilation controversies and other Irish/German tensions in the late nine-teenth century. However, the classicists regarded the American Catholic immigrant saga as essentially a story of success: while the Church in Europe was losing the working class during the Indus-trial Revolution, American Catholicism, against the historical odds and in the face of vicious nativist opposition, brokered the passage of ten million immigrants into mainstream American society while retaining the religious loyalties of the overwhelming majority of these new citizens. Moreover, according to the standard account, that "success" was reconfirmed in the post–World War II period, when Catholicism was transformed from a working-class, urban-based church into a middle- and upper-middle-class church demo-graphically centered on the suburbs.

The revisionists, on the other hand, cannot seem to bring them-selves to regard what they style the "ghetto Church" as the platform for any sort of success, religious, intellectual, or political. They accept, without much cavil, one of John Tracy Ellis's more dubious claims, viz., that American Catholicism had no intellectual life to speak of in the mid-1950s.[23] They ignore, perhaps because they hold in contempt, the political success of the urban Catholic Irish, Italians, Germans, and Poles. They have little to say, perhaps because the data ill fit their historiographic image, about the fact that American Catholicism during this "ghetto" period produced great pioneers of the liturgical and social-action movements like Vergil Michel. Nor do they account for the fact that the Thomism they dismissively deprecate (while failing to recognize the variant schools within the Thomist family) was taken seriously as an intellectual tradition by such respected secular scholars as Robert Maynard Hutchins and Mark Van Doren. Nor do they tell us why the "ghetto Church" attracted converts like Dorothy Day and Thomas Merton.[24] According to Wills and Dolan, only in the 1960s, when American Catholicism, personified by Daniel and

Philip Berrigan, definitively broke with the "ghetto Church" and its flag-waving patriotism, did it become possible to reclaim, again and at last, the "republican" heritage betrayed by John Carroll and (most of) his successors.[25]

Here, yet again, the revisionists have leaped from a valid historical point to an invalid historiographical conclusion. Of course there were strains of xenophobia in the immigrant Church, and some of them perdured into the 1960s. No one who reads Cardinal Lawrence Shehan's memoirs, in which he poignantly recalls being booed by masses of Catholic parishioners in 1966 when he testified before the Baltimore City Council in favor of an open-housing ordinance, can fail to realize that there were ugly elements in urban ethnic Catholicism.[26] But, and as Thomas Spalding himself demonstrates in *The Premier See*, the "ghetto Church" that produced racist parishioners also produced the priests and laity who were at the forefront of Baltimore's integration movement in the 1950s and 1960s.

Moreover, the revisionist account scarcely does justice to the immense vitality of Catholic life in, say, the Baltimore of Archbishop Michael J. Curley (1921–47) or the Chicago of Cardinal George Mundelein (1916–39).[27] Spalding, in *The Premier See,* seems baffled, charmed, repelled, and deeply impressed, concurrently, by Archbishop Curley and the church he led. Curley, Spalding insists, had "little use for the values of mainstream America" (what those values are is left to the reader's imagination), and deliberately eschewed the Carroll/Gibbons tradition for a church guided by "the myth of majestic changelessness." On the other hand, Spalding writes that Curley, with his "boldness and vigor," was "without doubt the most open, honest, and outspoken member of the American hierarchy" during that inter-war period.[28] What accounts for this curiously bifocal judgment? I suspect it may be due to the fact that Spalding, who has long and historic family connections in Baltimore, is somewhat less a revisionist on this matter of the "ghetto Church" than Dolan or Wills, and yet feels required to tip his historiographic hat at least modestly in that direction. Thus do intellectual fashions shape, posthumously, the reputations of great men.[29]

The Myopia of Present-Mindedness

The revisionist deprecation of John Carroll and the even more lurid revisionist portrait of the "ghetto Church" are not simply matters of intellectual fashion, however. They are interpretations deeply, even determinatively, influenced by contemporary church politics. To construct a historical foundation for the "progressive" Catholic agenda they champion today, Jay Dolan and others in the liberal Catholic opinion establishment have to make several moves. First, they must distinguish the "bad John Carroll" from the "good John Carroll." Second, they must show that the "bad Carroll" skewed the growth of American Catholicism, away from its "republican" roots and towards ultramontanism. (Gibbons and Ireland must be chuckling in heaven over the thought that they were closet ultramontanes, but revisionist historiography permits few calibrations to the right of Catholic Congregationalism.) Third, they must demonstrate that the net result of Carroll's betrayal was the "Catholic ghetto," whose evils must be catalogued in gory detail. Finally, they have to present the Second Vatican Council exclusively as the Council of *aggiornamento* ("updating"), rather than as the Council of an *aggiornamento* rooted in *ressourcement* (a "return to the sources"): including, it should be added, a return (in the Declaration on Religious Freedom) to the sources of authentic American Catholic liberalism in Carroll and Gibbons.

None of this, in its parts or as a whole, makes for an especially plausible or persuasive portrait of the American Catholic experience—unless one adopts what Frederick Crews has described as the "perpetually scandalized relation to the past" of "post-sixties conformism."[30] And that, alas, is a tough but accurate description of those revisionist Catholic historians who are working diligently to rewrite the American Catholic story line in order to prop up the sagging cause of "progressive" Catholicism today. These new historians of American Catholicism have, let it be freely admitted, opened some important windows of understanding. And doubtless some of their post-sixties conformism is less a matter of an ideological agenda than of unexamined assumptions. But what might be called, with due respect, the "Jay Dolan Project" in American Catholic history is of a different magnitude entirely. For it is an intepretation of history intellectually rooted in what Philip Gleason has aptly described as "more fundamental changes in *theological* outlook." The Dolan Project, in other words, is much less a matter of new facts than of new interpretive filters, of "a tendency to endorse as theological liberalism what the old [historiography] endorsed as social and procedural liberalism."[31]

The proper analogy, again, is to the revisionist school of American historiography in the 1960s. As William Appleman Williams deliberately sought to reshape and radicalize U.S. foreign policy through a revisionist (and essentially Marxist) reading of the history of America's encounter with the world, so Jay Dolan has, with energy and imagination, sought to buttress the "progressive" agenda in contemporary American Catholicism and the cause of an "independent American Catholic Church" by a radical retelling of the story. No doubt new light will be shed on the American Catholic experience as the Dolan school continues its work. But if the Williams analogy holds over the next decade, Professor Dolan and his colleagues may be in for an unwelcome surprise. For the net result of the revisionist/classicist battle over the origins of the Cold War was a strengthening of Harry Truman's posthumous claim to historical greatness—precisely the "myth" that the revisionists were most eager to debunk. Might the same be the happy fate of John Carroll and the Carroll Church when the debate over the Dolan Project runs its course?

ENRICHING THE CLASSIC STORY LINE:
A RESEARCH AGENDA

The new interest among American Catholic intellectuals in the history of their Church in the United States need not become the occasion for another set-piece ideological battle. The revisionists' claims must be met; but meeting them requires amplifying and extending, not simply replicating, the Shea/Guilday/Ellis story line. The following notes are intended as an illustrative (and certainly not exhaustive) probe towards a research agenda for the 1990s, and perhaps beyond.

1. The Americanist Controversy. Given that the term "American Catholicism" has itself become a point of controversy, what with "progressives" making it into a code word for a church "indepen-dent" of Rome and "restorationists" regarding it as tantamount to Gallicanism *redivivus*, it is surely long past time for a thorough, one-volume study of the "Americanist" controversy.

Considerable research has been done on this period over the past fifteen years. The trick will be to capture the originality of theolog-ical and spiritual insight among the Americanists—especially Isaac Hecker—without twisting these complex men into uni-dimensional precursors of the *National Catholic Reporter* sensibility. Margaret Mary Reher demonstrated some years ago that the "phantom heresy" label, adopted by the Gibbons party and later canonized by the creators of the classic story line, was far from satisfactory because it did not take account of the Americanists' originality on matters of ecclesiology and church/state relations.[32] Now that their position on church and state has been vindicated by a general council of the Church, it ought to be possible to take up the ecclesiological issue without reading (or better, rereading) the Americanists through the prism of a preference for what I referred to above as Catholic Congregationalism.

2. The National Conference of Catholic Bishops. In his recent *Arch-bishop: Inside the Power Structure of the American Catholic Church*,[33] Thomas J. Reese tried to give the intelligent lay reader a window into the process by which Catholic bishops in the United States are chosen, and into the work (local, national, and international) that the more senior among them actually do. It's a workmanlike and thorough job, and if Reese's personal sympathies lie with what might be called the "Bernardin party" in the American hierarchy, they don't intrude offensively into his analysis. Those tempted by the book's subtitle to expect juicy, inside dope are apt to be disappointed, however, by Father Reese's straightforward, social-science style.

More to the point of this essay, Father Reese doesn't give us the relevant history of the bishops' attempts to organize themselves on a national basis in order to pursue their ministry more effectively. Surely the debate over the American Catholic future (indeed the debate over the future of national episcopal conferences in Roman Catholicism) would benefit from a solid institutional history of the old National Catholic Welfare Conference and its successors, the National Conference of Catholic Bishops and the United States Catholic Conference.

Finding a historian who can rise above the controversies that surround the NCCB/USCC complex will be no easy business, but twenty-five years after the creation of these bodies, the time seems right for an honest telling of the tale of their origins, and a careful appraisal of their impact on both the life of the American Church and its interface with American political culture. Is it true, as their defenders would have it, that the NCCB/USCC dyad continues, in contemporary form, the conciliar and consultative tradition of American Catholicism that gave rise to the seven provincial and three plenary councils of Baltimore—the fullest expression of collegiality in nineteenth-century Roman Catholicism anywhere in the world? Or, as some critics charge, did Cardinal John Dearden's decision to follow an American corporate model in organizing the NCCB/USCC after Vatican II create a bureaucratic imbroglio that in fact led to a less open, more restricted conversation within the American Church on issues bearing both on its internal life and on its address to matters of public policy?[34] Sorting through such basic questions of appraisal is going to be very difficult until the detailed history of the NCCB/USCC and its predecessor NCWC is known.

3. The Liturgical Movement. American Catholicism in the twentieth century has been shaped by a variety of movements, few of which have been given adequate historical study. The liturgical movement of the 1930s, 1940s, and 1950s has probably had a more direct impact on the lives of ordinary American Catholics than any other such enterprise; there is, however, no fully detailed, sympathetic, and yet critical appraisal of this phenomenon, its successes and its failures.

Viewed from one angle, liturgical renewal in American Catholicism has been a striking success: the overwhelming majority of American Catholics evidence no interest in a return to the Tridentine rite, and seem generally pleased with the liturgical reforms of Vatican II. One can hardly suggest, however, that parish liturgies across the United States are characterized by aesthetic care, as the virtually uncontested triumph of the hateful, throw-away "missalette" demonstrates. Why, twenty-five years after the Council, has American Catholicism failed to produce a single hymnal of distinction? Why are the prayer-texts of the liturgy translated into such abysmal English? Why is preaching in such desperate straits in the American Church? Why haven't new forms of eucharistic piety arisen as the old forms (Benediction, Forty Hours' Devotion, and the like) collapsed? At a different level of debate, why were the links between liturgy and social action (on which the pioneers like Father Vergil Michel insisted) never forged, beyond a small elite? And why did the elite Liturgical Conference, itself the main organizing instrument of the movement, dissipate into radical-chic politics in the late 1960s? All these questions seem well worth exploring with care.

4. *Greats.* These are, admittedly, institution- and issue-focused concerns. If American Catholicism is to seize what Richard John Neuhaus and others have called this "Catholic moment" in the ongoing drama of the American democratic experiment, more than institutional self-understanding will be required. American Catholics, like any other body of people called to a great task in history, need heroes. And therefore I would suggest that it is time to revive the tradition of great biographies in American Catholicism—a revival we may hope was presaged, as noted above, by the 1988 publication of Marvin O'Connell's *John Ireland and the American Catholic Church.*

There is no shortage of large-scale figures of whom modern biographies would be entirely welcome. John Carroll, the first of the line, is also first on this list. The most recent full-length biography of Carroll was written in 1955, twenty-one years *before* the *John Carroll Papers* were published by the University of Notre Dame Press. A major biographical study of the founding father is certainly in order, not least because of the current revisionist/classicist controversy over the Carroll legacy.

A twentieth-century exponent of the Carroll/Gibbons Church, Cardinal Edward Mooney of Detroit, is another of the great unstudied figures of American Catholic history. Mooney's career was immensely varied and interesting: apostolic delegate to India and Japan, bishop of Rochester, archbishop of Detroit; power broker within the NCWC, and between the NCWC and the Vatican; an internationalist, a pioneer ecumenist, and a leader of the moderate-to-liberal wing of the pre-Conciliar American hierarchy for almost twenty years. A study of Mooney's life and concerns might well help establish that the Carroll Church continued to germinate—in men like Martin John Spalding and the Detroit prelate—far beyond the time when the revisionists consign it to the junk heap of ecclesiastical history.

Finally, it is long past time for a thorough biographical study of the life and thought of Father John Courtney Murray, S.J.[35] Like Carroll, Murray is now a figure of considerable controversy. A vigorous hermeneutic battle for the Murray legacy is under way among American Catholic intellectuals, with a revisionist school arguing that Murray (to reverse the revisionist interpretation of Carroll!) got radicalized under the influence of Bernard Lonergan in his later years, and became a kind of precursor to Richard P. McBrien and Charles Curran on the contemporary American Catholic scene.[36] Murray classicists find this implausible in the extreme, and thus the interpretive battle is engaged. Conducting the new quest for the historical Murray and preparing a full-scale Murray biography will be no easy task: the Murray papers are in a largely disorganized (some would say, disgraceful) condition at the Georgetown University Library. But as Murray looms ever larger as a central figure in the debate over Catholicism and the American democratic experiment, a classically biographical study of his life and thought is very much needed.

CONCLUDING UNSCIENTIFIC POSTSCRIPT

"History is an antidote to despair," or so thought a college teacher of mine. Perhaps he would pardon my amending his *mot* to read, "History is an antidote to frivolity."

American Catholicism suffers from an excess of frivolity in the opening years of its third century. A church that is the largest voluntary association in the country; a church whose universal pastor has, over the past decade, definitively answered Stalin's cynical query about the pope's divisions; a church that is, demographically, at its strongest historical point of leverage in American society—this is a church that would seem well positioned to seize a possible "Catholic moment" in American history, *pro Deo et patria*.

Instead, the "Catholic moment" proposition has been subjected to the death of a thousand cuts from both opinion establishments, the liberal and the conservative, in the American Church. The left refuses to concede the possibility of a "Catholic moment" built around the post-modern ministry of Pope John Paul II. The right insists that the *real* "Catholic moment" was in the heyday of Archbishop Curley, when the "myth of majestic changelessness" prevailed against all the Church's enemies, foreign and domestic.[37]

Simply paying more attention to The Story of American Catholicism will not solve the problem of Catholic frivolity in the 1990s. Indeed, if the revisionists come to dominate the field, their scandalized relationship to the past ("I thank thee, O God, that I am not like my ancestors: racist, sexist, warmongering, environmentally insensitive, subservient to Rome," etc., etc.) virtually guarantees more frivolity, now extended back across several generations.

On the other hand, a renewed and amplified classic story line could revivify the "Catholic moment" proposition in several ways. It could help distinguish what is authentically "American Catholic" from what is merely post-sixties conformism. It could suggest models (Carroll, Gibbons, Murray) for the interaction between the United States and Rome that mediate between Catholic Congregationalism and the tendency to see Catholicism in the United States as a mere branch office of Roman Catholic Church, Inc. It might put to rest one of the least plausible feminist claims about the pre-Conciliar Church, viz., that it was an institution in which women were "disempowered."[38] It would, in sum, usefully complexify the current Catholic debate, and thus create the possibility of moving that debate to a more adult level of discussion.

Whom you would change, you must first love, taught Martin Luther King, Jr. Whom you would love, you must first know, because love is an act of the intellect as well as of the emotions. The new historiography of American Catholicism teaches, sometimes subtly and sometimes overtly, a contempt for the Catholic past, and indeed for the American past: which seems a dubious base on which to build the American Catholicism of the future. But neither can an American Catholicism capable of seizing a possible "Catholic moment" be built on the receding sands of a forgotten past.

Any possible "Catholic moment" in American history will combine, as did the Second Vatican Council, a strategy of *aggiornamento* with a strategy of *ressourcement*. And that, it seems, is what the Carroll Church tried to do, at least in the standard account of The Story of American Catholicism. Amplifying and refining that classic story line is thus an important intellectual exercise for the Church today. And it just might be, as well, both an antidote to despair and a source of good cheer about the future.

Notes

CHAPTER ONE
Religious Freedom

1. *Declaration on Religious Freedom*, #2.
2. Paul Johnson, *Modern Times* (New York: Harper and Row, 1983), pp. 50–51.
3. *Laborem Exercens*, #6.
4. *Dives in Misericordia*, #11.
5. *Redemptor Hominis*, #17.
6. "Instruction on Christian Freedom and Liberation," #95.
7. James V. Schall, *The Church, the State, and Society in the Thought of John Paul II* (Chicago: Franciscan Herald Press, 1982), p. 50.
8. Address to the ambassador of Senegal, 2 December 1978.
9. Address to the president of Ghana, 8 May 1980.
10. Schall, *The Church, the State, and Society*, p. 57.
11. *New York Times*, 3 April 1987.
12. "Address to the XXXIV General Assembly of the United Nations Organization," 2 October 1979, p. 19.
13. John Murray Cuddihy, *No Offense: Civil Religion and Protestant Taste* (New York: Seabury, 1978).
14. Stanley Hauerwas, "The Importance of Being Catholic: A Protestant View," *First Things*, March 1990.

CHAPTER TWO
Catholicism and Democracy

1. From *Mirari Vos*, as cited and discussed in Roger Aubert et al., *History of the Church VIII: The Church Between Revolution and Restoration* (New York: Crossroad, 1981), pp. 286–92. The historical and sociological context of Gregory XVI's condemnation is well summarized by Rodger Charles, S.J.:

Gregory XVI was a temporal ruler faced with a revolt in his own dominions, a revolt which was in the name of a liberalism which . . . was in practice anticlerical and anti-Christian. . . . The Pope could not accept state indifferentism in matters of religion, nor grant liberty of conscience while these implied positive anti-clerical and anti-Christian attitudes. Liberty of the press and separation of the Church and the state were likewise rejected absolutely because of their secularist implications. *This was the essence of the papal dilemma: popes, as vicars of Christ, could hardly recommend policies which, if put into practice in their own states, would link them [i.e., the popes] with men and ideas both anti-clerical and anti-religious.* Only when the question of temporal power of the papacy had been solved . . . could the situation satisfactorily be resolved [*The Social Teaching of Vatican II* (San Francisco: Ignatius Press, 1982), p. 239, emphasis added].

2. For a portrait of Pius IX that usefully complexifies many of the regnant stereotypes, cf. E.E.Y. Hales, *Pio Nono: A Study in European Politics and Religion in the Nineteenth Century* (London: Eyre and Spottiswoode, 1954).

3. The Holy See was not, of course, alone in this judgment, although the logic of concern varied from institution to institution. Cf. Henry A. Kissinger, *A World Restored: Metternich, Castlereagh and the Problems of Peace, 1812–1822* (Boston: Houghton Mifflin, 1973).

4. For a discussion of this point, cf. John Courtney Murray, *We Hold These Truths: Catholic Reflections on the American Proposition* (New York: Doubleday Image Books, 1964), pp. 40 ff. The danger in question was encapsulated in the Abbé Sieyes's defense of the replacement of the old States-General by the revolutionary National Assembly: "The nation exists before all, it is the origin of everything, it is the law itself." Cited in Conor Cruise O'Brien, "A Lost Chance to Save the Jews?," *New York Review of Books*, April 27, 1989, p. 27. O'Brien correctly identifies the Jacobin current as the forerunner of twentieth-century totalitarianism, and chillingly cites the German theologian Gerhard Kittel, a "moderate," who wrote in 1933, in *Die Judenfrage*, that " 'Justice' is not an abstraction but something which grows out of the blood and soil and history of a *Volk*." O'Brien could, of course, have cited any number of Leninist *mots* to this effect, too.

5. Pope Pius VII (1800–23) was an interesting countercase. Despite his personal suffering at the hands of Napoleon, Pius VII was not so thoroughly soured on the liberal project as his successors Leo XII, Gregory XVI, and Pius IX. As Cardinal Luigi Barnaba Chiaramonti, Pius VII was a compromise candidate at the conclave of 1800, but one who had shown his moderate colors at Christmas 1797, when he shocked his conservative congregants with a sermon in which he declared there was no necessary conflict between Christianity and democracy. As pope, Pius VII and his secretary of state, the brilliant Cardinal Ercole Consalvi, tried to "blend administrative, judicial, and financial reforms on the liberal French model with the antiquated papal system"—an effort at cross-breeding that "exasperated reactionaries and progressives alike, and led to serious revolts" (J.N.D. Kelly, *The Oxford Dictionary of Popes* [Oxford: Oxford University Press, 1986], pp. 302–4). Pius VII's modest reforms were rolled back by his successor, Leo XII (1823–29), who also took up again the rhetorical cudgels against liberalism. Thus ended what might be called the Chiaramonti/Consalvi experiment in rapprochement between Roman Catholicism and the liberalizing reforms of the day. For the next fifty years, conservative retrenchment would dominate Vatican policy, and the notion of conservative reform pioneered by Pius VII and Consalvi would fall by the wayside.

6. Cf. Owen Chadwick, *The Secularization of the European Mind in the Nineteenth Century* (Cambridge: Cambridge University Press, 1975).

7. Arthur Schlesinger, Sr., once told the dean of American Catholic historians,

John Tracy Ellis, that "I regard the prejudice against your Church as the deepest bias in the history of the American people." Cited in John Tracy Ellis, *American Catholicism*, 2nd ed., rev. (Chicago: University of Chicago Press, 1969), p. 151.

8. John Tracy Ellis, ed., *Documents of American Catholic History*, vol. 2 (Wilmington: Michael Glazier, 1987), pp. 462–63 (emphasis added).

9. Gerald P. Fogarty, S.J., *The Vatican and the American Hierarchy from 1870 to 1965* (Wilmington: Michael Glazier, 1985), p. 41.

10. *Longinqua Oceani*, in Ellis, *Documents of American Catholic History*, vol. 2, p. 502.

11. Cf. Anthony Rhodes, *The Vatican in the Age of the Dictators, 1922–1945* (New York: Holt, Rinehart and Winston, 1973), pp. 14–15.

12. Jacques Maritain, *Christianity and Democracy* (San Francisco: Ignatius Press, 1986). Maritain had an interesting historical perspective on the events through which he was living, in exile in the United States:

We are looking on at the liquidation of what is known as the "modern world" which ceased to be modern a quarter of a century ago when the First World War marked its entry into the past. The question is: in what will this liquidation result? . . . [T]he tremendous historical fund of energy and truth accumulated for centuries is still available to human freedom, the forces of renewal are on the alert and it is still up to us to make sure that this catastrophe of the modern world is not a regression to a perverted aping of the Ancient Regime or of the Middle Ages and that it does not wind up in the totalitarian putrefaction of the German New Order. It is up to us rather to see that it emerges in a new and truly creative age, where man, in suffering and hope, will resume his journey toward the conquest of freedom [pp. 11, 17].

13. The divisions in pre-war French society are well captured, in fictional form, in Piers Paul Read, *The Free Frenchman* (New York: Ivy Books, 1986).

14. One should also note, with an eye to 1992, the connection between these national Christian Democratic movements and the movement for West European integration that led to the Common Market and the European Parliament.

15. Cited in Joseph A. Komonchak, "Subsidiarity in the Church: The State of the Question," *The Jurist* 48 (1988), p. 299.

16. Is there a connection between the principle of subsidiarity and the American concept of federalism here? It would be going considerably out of bounds to suggest that Madison's concept of federalism, as suggested in "Federalist 10" and "Federalist 51," was informed by that classic Catholic social theory which eventually evolved the principle of subsidiarity; Madison should not be taken as a kind of proto–Pius XI. Indeed, "Federalist 10" and "Federalist 51" endorse decentralized decision-making, not as an expression of human possibility, but as a remedy for human defects (the defect of faction).

On the other hand, one can argue that federal arrangements (irrespective of their political-philosophical rationale) are one possible expression, in history, of the principle of subsidiarity. One could possibly go further, and suggest that the principle of subsidiarity establishes a firmer moral-cultural and indeed philosophical foundation for federal arrangements than Madison's "let a thousand factions bloom," so to speak, that no one of them may become oppressively dominant. Grounded as it is in an ontology of the person that links *being* and *acting*, and that regards human community as rooted in the social nature of the human person, the principle of subsidiarity might provide a more satisfactory basis for federalism

154 NOTES TO PAGES 36–47

than the voluntarism with which Madison is (wrongfully, in my view) often charged, and of which some of his successors in American political theory (principally the "progressivist" historians of the Parrington/Beard school) are surely guilty.

17. These definitions, as well as the schema above, are adapted from Komonchak, "Subsidiarity in the Church."

18. On the Königswinterer Kreis, cf. Franz H. Mueller, *The Church and the Social Question* (Washington: American Enterprise Institute, 1984), pp. 116–17.

19. On this distinction between the two encyclicals, cf. Mueller, *The Church and the Social Question*, p. 114.

20. Cf. George Weigel, "John Courtney Murray and the Catholic Human Rights Revolution," *This World* 15 (Fall 1986), pp. 14–27.

21. For a detailed examination of the Murray/Fenton/Connell controversy, cf. Donald Pelotte, *John Courtney Murray: Theologian in Conflict* (New York: Paulist Press, 1975).

22. George Weigel, *Catholicism and the Renewal of American Democracy* (New York: Paulist Press, 1989), p. 86.

23. *Dignitatis Humanae Personae*, #2.

24. Ibid. (emphasis added).

25. Chief among these "prior" social institutions and the fundamental values they incarnate are what Murray called the *res sacrae in temporalibus*, those "sacred things in man's secular life" of which the Church had been the traditional guardian:

> Man's relation to God and to the Church, the inner unity of human personality as citizen and Christian but one man, the integrity of the human body, the husband-wife relationship, the political obligation, the moral values inherent in economic and cultural activity as aspects of human life, the works of justice and charity which are the necessary expressions of the Christian and human spirit, and finally that patrimony of ideas which are the basis of civilized life—the ideas of law and right, of political power and the obligations of citizenship, of property, etc. [John Courtney Murray, "Paul Blanshard and the New Nativism," *The Month* (new series) 5:4 (April 1951), p. 224].

26. For a fuller discussion of the interior and public meanings of religious freedom, see the preceding chapter, "Religious Freedom: The First Human Right."

27. John Courtney Murray, S.J., "The Issue of Church and State at Vatican Council II," *Theological Studies* 27:4 (December 1966), p. 586.

28. For a fuller discussion of the instruction, and references, cf. my *Tranquillitas Ordinis: The Present Failure and Future Promise of American Catholic Thought on War and Peace* (New York: Oxford University Press, 1987), pp. 291 ff.

29. "Instruction on Certain Aspects of the 'Theology of Liberation,' " #17.

30. "Instruction on Christian Freedom and Liberation," #95.

31. *Sollicitudo Rei Socialis*, #16.

32. Ibid., #44.

33. Ibid.

34. Ibid.

35. Quoted in the *New York Times*, April 6, 1987.

36. Cited in *Origins* 17, no. 15 (Sept. 25, 1987).

37. Joseph Ratzinger, "Europe: A Heritage with Obligations for Christians,"

in *Church, Ecumenism and Politics* (New York: Crossroad, 1988), pp. 228–29, 234.

38. "Instruction on Christian Freedom and Liberation," #6.

39. William Lee Miller, *The First Liberty: Religion and the American Republic* (New York: Knopf, 1986), pp. 145–46.

40. For the Catholic tradition of "moderate realism" in social ethics, cf. my *Tranquillitas Ordinis*, pp. 25–45.

41. See "The Jacobin Temptation in American Catholicism—The Worlds of the *National Catholic Reporter*," in my *Catholicism and the Renewal of American Democracy*, pp. 47–69.

42. *New York Times*, July 27, 1988.

43. Such a second- or third-phase liberation theology would also have to address the liberation of Latin American economies, and individual Latin Americans, from the crushing weight of mercantilist regulation and bureaucracy. One important test of the reality of a second- or third-phase liberation theology will be its openness to the analysis and prescriptions of, say, Hernando de Soto in *The Other Path* (New York: Harper & Row, 1989). One point of connection between de Soto's empirical studies on entrepreneurship and the evolution of Catholic social teaching may be found in *Sollicitudo Rei Socialis*, where John Paul II defends the "right of economic initiative" as an essential component of integral human development.

44. The term is defined by Eugene Hillman as follows:

> Inculturation . . . refers to the central and dynamic principle governing the Christian missionary outreach to peoples not yet evangelized, or among whom the church is not yet rooted firmly and indigenously. More commonly, this is known as the principle of catholicity, or accommodation, or adaptation, or indigenization, or contextualization. . . . [T]he principle of inculturation may be traced to its earliest articulation in St. Paul's great debate with the Jewish Christians [who] . . . erroneously confused their new faith with their own ethnic conventions, cultural practices and local laws which they wished to impose upon all non-Jewish converts to Christianity. . . . [In contemporary terms, the principle means that if the Church] is to become a universally visible and intelligible sign of humankind's unity and salvation . . . [it] must learn to experience and express itself through the cultural riches not only of Western peoples but of all peoples [Eugene Hillman, "Inculturation," in Joseph A. Komonchak, Mary Collins, and Dermot A. Lane, eds., *The New Dictionary of Theology* (Wilmington: Michael Glazier, 1987), pp. 510–12].

CHAPTER THREE
The "Tranquillitas Ordinis" Debate

1. New York: Oxford University Press, 1987.

2. Jay P. Dolan, "Defining the Good Fight," *New York Times Book Review*, April 26, 1987.

3. Robert Gilliam, *The Catholic Worker*, December 1987.

4. Peter Steinfels, "The Heritage Abandoned? George Weigel Explains It All," *Commonweal*, September 11 and 25, 1987.

5. David Hollenbach, S.J., "War and Peace in American Catholic Thought: A Heritage Abandoned?," *Theological Studies* 48:4 (December 1987).

6. Avery Dulles, S.J., *Crisis*, July-August 1987.

7. Hollenbach, "War and Peace," p. 711.

8. I freely concede that I was thinking in terms of decades, not years, here, and I am delighted to confess my imaginative myopia in thinking about how soon the Communist empire in central eastern Europe might break down. On the other hand, I at least admitted the possibility of the Communist crackup, which is more than could be said for many of my friends and adversaries, left and right.

9. Andrew Sullivan, in the middle of a rather Kierkegaardian review of *TO* in the flagship journal of American liberalism, thought that I had at least gotten this right:

> [Weigel's] argument that [natural law and the statecraft implicit in just-war theory have] been culpably neglected by a Catholic hierarchy more concerned with neo-Marxist understandings of "structural sin," or with neo-Pelagian understandings of the possibility of a world without nuclear weapons, is powerful and convincing. He reminds us of how facile much of the debate about war and peace has been, of how simple references to uninterpreted scripture have been the norm, of how easy it has been to let questions of secular policy usurp the commitment to a comprehensive and sustained vision of the Catholic understanding of peace. He is particularly acute in his analysis of how the Catholic conception of peace as a political construction was ceded in Vietnam to arguments that were part of, rather than a curative for, the public trauma. . . . And he correctly remarks upon the tactics of extremists, noticeably Pax Christi, in manipulating the necessity for Church unity by forcing the Bishops' Conference to move left or face open division ["Cross Purposes," *The New Republic*, June 1, 1987, p. 33].

10. This absurd labeling continues, alas, into the 1990s, as exemplified in Phillip Berryman's recent effort, *Our Unfinished Business: The U.S. Catholic Bishops' Letters on Peace and the Economy* (New York: Pantheon, 1990). Berryman's further claim that my analysis of the thought of Father J. Bryan Hehir was motivated by "envy" (p. 60) is the zenith of silliness. Earlier, Gary Bullert, from the other (i.e., far right) end of the ideological spectrum, had suggested that *TO* was an effort on my part to grab Father Hehir's job! (Cf. "A Neo-Conservative Catholic on War and Peace," *The Wanderer*, June 18,1987.)

11. *The Challenge of Peace*, draft 2, in *Origins* 12:20 (Oct. 28, 1982), p. 312.

12. Hollenbach, "War and Peace," p. 720.

13. Ibid., p. 721.

14. On the human rights–security nexus in U.S.-Soviet relations, cf. Carol O'Hallaron, "Risky Business: Linking Human Rights and Defence Issues at the Vienna CSCE," *Cambridge Review of International Affairs* 4:1 (Spring 1990), pp. 27–39.

15. Hollenbach cited the early Carter administration as an example of a circumstance in which "the effort to advance human rights . . . jeopardize[d] arms control in a serious way" ("War and Peace," p. 720). Other observers argue that it was the nature of the Carter deep-cut proposals in March 1977 that angered the Soviets and untracked the SALT II negotiation. When one combines that plausible alternative view with the (equally plausible) assertion that SALT II didn't really constitute a major arms-control achievement, Hollenbach's criticism begins to look weak indeed.

16. Hollenbach, "War and Peace," p. 725.

17. David Hollenbach, S.J., "Ethical Principles, Strategic Policy, and the Catholic Bishops: The Continuing Argument," lecture at the Catholic University of America, October 27, 1989, p. 24. Hollenbach goes on to suggest that the bishops' 1988 "report" on *The Challenge of Peace* "effectively remedied" the 1983 pastoral letter's "vulnerability on this score." Be that as it may, the basic point remains that the pastoral letter failed to place the nuclear-weapons debate within the appropriate political and strategic context.

Later in his Catholic University lecture, Hollenbach suggested that "there is now at least a realistic possibility that the threat of nuclear war and the denial of human rights can be simultaneously reduced," and noted that "this would open an avenue toward possibly greater consensus between the bishops and critics like Weigel" (p. 27). That is true; and such a consensus would affirm, in practice if not in theory, the "linkage" proposals made in *Tranquillitas Ordinis*.

18. Hollenbach, "War and Peace," p. 712.

19. Avery Dulles, S.J., *Crisis*, July-August 1987, p. 49.

20. Cf. Matthew Murphy, *Betraying the Bishops* (Washington: Ethics and Public Policy Center, 1987). Murphy's book is far more concerned with arms-control minutiae than I am, but his description of the tendentious readings of *The Challenge of Peace* that now shape many educational programs is an important cautionary tale.

21. Cited in *Tranquillitas Ordinis*, p. 166.

CHAPTER FOUR
Camels and Needles, Talents and Treasure

1. Cf., for example, the Carrolls' correspondence with George Washington on the latter's inauguration as first president under the Constitution of 1787, in John Tracy Ellis, ed., *Documents of American Catholic History*, vol. 1 (Wilmington: Michael Glazier, 1987), pp. 169–72.

2. On spirituality in Catholic Maryland, cf. Jay Dolan, *The American Catholic Experience* (New York: Doubleday, 1985), pp. 80–97; Joseph P. Chinnici, O.F.M., *Living Stones: The History and Structure of Catholic Spiritual Life in the United States* (New York: Macmillan, 1989), pp. 26–34.

3. Cf. Richard Shaw, *Dagger John: The Unquiet Life and Times of Archbishop John Hughes of New York* (New York: Paulist Press, 1977), for an extended portrait of this remarkable figure.

4. John Hughes, "A Lecture on the Importance of a Christian Basis for the Science of Political Economy, and Its Application to the Affairs of Life," in Patrick W. Carey, ed., *American Catholic Religious Thought* (New York: Paulist Press, 1987), pp. 202–3. Hughes's lecture was delivered to the Calvert Institute in Baltimore and the Carroll Institute of Philadelphia on January 17–18, 1844.

5. Orestes Brownson, "The Laboring Class," *The Boston Quarterly Review*, vol. 3, cited in John J. Mitchell, *Critical Voices in American Catholic Economic Thought* (New York: Paulist Press, 1989), p. 8.

6. Ibid., p. 20.

7. Ibid.

8. Ibid., p. 9.

9. Cf. ibid., p. 18.

10. Ibid, p. 19.

11. Ibid.

12. For a succinct summary of the McGlynn Affair, cf. Gerald P. Fogarty, S.J., *The Vatican and the American Hierarchy from 1870 to 1965* (Wilmington: Michael Glazier, 1985), pp. 93–114.

13. Cf. Marvin R. O'Connell, *John Ireland and the American Catholic Church* (St. Paul: Minnesota Historical Society, 1988), pp. 378 ff.

14. Details may be found in Fogarty, *The Vatican and the American Hierarchy*, pp. 87–92.

15. Ibid., p. 91.

16. Cited ibid., p. 238.

17. Ibid., p. 237. For a more complete analysis of the Bishops' Program, see Joseph M. McShane, S.J., *"Sufficiently Radical": Catholicism, Progressivism, and the Bishops' Program of 1919* (Washington: Catholic University of America Press, 1986).

18. McShane, *"Sufficiently Radical,"* p. 199.

19. Cited in Fogarty, *The Vatican and the American Hierarchy*, p. 238.

20. Dennis McCann, "Option for the Poor: Rethinking a Catholic Tradition," in Richard John Neuhaus, ed., *The Preferential Option for the Poor* (Grand Rapids: Eerdmans, 1988), p. 51.

21. The most prominent example of this kind of analysis is, of course, Michael Novak's *The Spirit of Democratic Capitalism* (New York: Simon and Schuster, 1982).

22. Cf. *Gaudium et Spes*, #63–72.

23. For an analysis of *Populorum Progressio*, cf. my *Catholicism and the Renewal of American Democracy* (New York: Paulist Press, 1989), pp. 174–78.

24. For an overview of the liberation-theology agenda and its impact on American Catholic thinking, cf. my *Tranquillitas Ordinis: The Present Failure and Future Promise of American Catholic Thought on War and Peace* (New York: Oxford University Press, 1987), pp. 286–300. Cf. also Michael Novak, *Will It Liberate? Questions for Liberation Theology* (New York: Paulist Press, 1987).

25. For a sympathetic analysis of Maurin's and Day's positions, and their roots in Maurin's Christian personalism (itself influenced by the French moral theologian Emmanuel Mounier), cf. William D. Miller, *A Harsh and Dreadful Love: Dorothy Day and the Catholic Worker Movement* (New York: Liveright, 1973).

26. Cf. Andrew M. Greeley, *The American Catholic: A Social Portrait* (New York: Basic Books, 1977).

27. Michael Novak has, again, been in the forefront of this discussion. Cf. *The Spirit of Democratic Capitalism*, chapter twenty; *Toward a Theology of the Corporation* (Washington: American Enterprise Institute, 1981); *The American Vision: An Essay on the Future of Democratic Capitalism* (Washington: American Enterprise Institute, 1981).

28. For an overview of the theory of the "new class," cf. Peter L. Berger, "Ethics and the Present Class Struggle," *Worldview*, April 1978, pp. 6–11.

29. For a portrait of some of the dominant currents of thought in the American Catholic "new class," cf. chapter three in my *Catholicism and the Renewal of American Democracy*.

30. This motivation has been hotly denied by those responsible for the official hermeneutics of *Economic Justice for All*, but I first heard it in personal conversation from Bishop Rosazza himself, who presumably knows what he, at least, was up to.

31. On this point, cf. Jim Castelli, *The Bishops and the Bomb: Waging Peace in a Nuclear Age* (Garden City: Doubleday Image Books, 1983), p. 15. Since Castelli's is a semi-official history of the 1983 pastoral, his judgment on this point, at least, is virtually unassailable.

32. *Economic Justice for All*, #30–55.

33. Ibid., #98.

34. Ibid., #117.

35. John Langan, S.J., "Afterword: A Direction for the Future," in Thomas M. Gannon, S.J., ed., *The Catholic Challenge to the American Economy: Reflections on the U.S. Bishops' Pastoral Letter on Catholic Social Teaching and the U.S. Economy* (New York: Macmillan, 1987), p. 264.

36. Some—Ernest van den Haag comes to mind—might argue that this "missed opportunity" in American Catholicism is primarily due to what is taken to be Rome's continued nervousness about, bordering on animus against, capitalism. Wrote van den Haag recently,

> The Roman Catholic Church . . . has always been allergic to economic reasoning. The love for the poor, the failures, the simpletons, the oppressed, and the degraded, which the Gospels so magnificently commend, has often turned into a love for poverty and failure, and—more important—into a hostility to success and wealth, and to a system that permits either. Yet the Gospels merely assign a low priority to worldly success. They are not hostile to it. Renunciation of the world is favored for the sake of one's soul. But merely being poor without having renounced anything is no virtue, any more than being rich without having deprived anybody is a vice. Helping is meritorious. Needing help is not [Ernest van den Haag, "The War Between Paleos and Neos," *National Review*, February 24, 1989, p. 23].

William McGurn's essay, "Preferential Option: Why Manila Is Poor and Hong Kong Is Rich" (*Crisis*, June 1989, pp. 27–32), argues, in a more extended fashion, that classic Roman economic thought suffers from "fundamentally materialist assumptions about economic life," and takes "an essentially managerial approach to wealth that ignores the infusion of human faith and creativity that brings it into being."

However one assesses the impact of the Roman magisterium's "allergy" to capitalism on the failure to develop an ethic and spirituality of wealth creation in American Catholicism—and I am inclined to think that the *least* one can say is that the magisterium did not encourage such a development—"Rome" seems an unlikely place to locate the ideological roots of the American Catholic new class's opposition to an ethic of wealth creation, for it is precisely over-against "Rome" that much of the current American Catholic intellectual and opinion establishment defines itself. Father Richard McBrien, for example, may find it titillating to cite *Sollicitudo Rei Socialis* in his polemics against Michael Novak, Richard Neuhaus, and me (cf. McBrien's column, "Encyclical Poses Complex Challenges," *Brooklyn Tablet*, April 16, 1988); but no one who has followed McBrien's writing carefully will think that he takes his economics, any more than he takes his moral theology, his ecclesiology, or his understanding of church/state relations, from Karol Wojtyla and Joseph Ratzinger.

The roots of the American Catholic new-class animus against capitalism lie in a variety of vulgarized-Marxist themes, which are then given a patina of respectability through the selective citation of Roman documents. In school we used to call that "eisegesis."

37. Cf. Gregory Baum, *The Priority of Labor: A Commentary on "Laborem Exercens"* (New York: Paulist Press, 1982).

38. Cf., for example, John Gray, "The Last Socialist?," *National Review*, June 30, 1989, pp. 27–29, 31.

39. *Sollicitudo Rei Socialis*, #15.

40. *Laborem Exercens*, #25.

41. The biblical warrant for this may be found in the parable of the talents (Matt. 25:14–30).

42. Lay Commission on Catholic Social Thought and the U.S. Economy, "Toward the Future: A Lay Letter," p. 28.

43. Cf., for example, *Sollicitudo Rei Socialis*, #42; *Economic Justice for All*, #87.

44. McCann, "Option for the Poor," pp. 37–44.

45. Ibid., p. 44.

46. Peter Berger, *The Capitalist Revolution* (New York: Basic Books, 1986).

47. Ralph McInerny, "Maritain In and On America," in Richard John Neuhaus, ed., *Reinhold Niebuhr Today* (Grand Rapids: Eerdmans, 1989), p. 37.

48. Jacques Maritain, *Reflections on America* (New York: Scribner, 1958), pp. 30, 33, 35.

49. Josef Pieper, *Leisure: The Basis of Culture* (New York: New American Library, 1963).

50. *Laborem Exercens*, preface and #25.

51. Gilbert Meilaender, "To Throw Oneself Into the Wave: The Problem of Possessions," in Neuhaus, ed., *The Preferential Option for the Poor*, pp. 79–80.

52. Ibid., p. 81.

CHAPTER FIVE
The Ecumenism of Time

1. Letter to "A," 2 August 1955, in Flannery O'Connor, *The Habit of Being: Letters of Flannery O'Connor*, ed. Sally Fitzgerald (New York: Farrar, Straus, Giroux, 1979), p. 92.

2. Letter to "A.," 9 August 1955, ibid., pp. 93–94.

3. Letter to "A.," 16 December 1955, ibid., pp. 124–25.

4. The question of "recognition" becomes an urgent one when Flannery O'Connor's approach to the faith that she believed central to her literary work is reduced to these terms, in a new study of American Catholic intellectual life: "O'Connor was critical of what she called the 'Catholic smugness' characteristic of the period. She complained about the 'vapid Catholicism' in which she had been reared. She believed that 'you have to save yourself from it some day or dry up' " (Margaret M. Reher, *Catholic Intellectual Life in America* [New York: Macmillan, 1989], p. 126).

5. "American Catholic intellectuals" covers a lot of territory, to be sure. I use the term here primarily in reference to the American Catholic theological community, to contemporary historians of American Catholicism, and, by extension, to those Catholic intellectuals whose professional interests include the application of Catholic social thought to the exigencies of public policy, or to an analysis of

the American socio-cultural scene. There are, obviously, a lot of "American Catholic intellectuals" who don't fit this profile. But these are the worlds of American Catholic intellectual life to which I pay the most attention, and about which I may have some "standing" (as the lawyers say) as a commentator.

6. For an analysis of just how significant a role-reversal this is, cf. the chapter "John Ireland's Dream" in my *Catholicism and the Renewal of American Democracy* (New York: Paulist Press, 1989). The modern *locus classicus* for the argument that Catholicism need not hang its head in shame before the bar of American modernity is, of course, John Courtney Murray's *We Hold These Truths*. A successor generation of Catholic social theorists criticized Murray for being too uncritical about the American experiment in democracy. But since the entire (and entirely radical) thrust of *We Hold These Truths* is to demonstrate that the American experiment lacks the kind of broadly accepted "public philosophy" capable of sustaining democratic pluralism, the critics, on this point at least, seem a bit off the mark.

7. Cf. Richard John Neuhaus's analysis of this point in *The Catholic Moment: The Paradox of the Church in the Postmodern World* (New York: Harper & Row, 1987). Neuhaus argues that this project of opening "the windows of the modern world to the worlds of which it is part" (p. 284), which preeminently include the world of transcendent Truth and Love, summarizes the "postmodern" thrust of the public ministry of John Paul II.

Peter Maurin, the Pied Piper philosopher of the Catholic Worker movement, was another figure with a sense of the "Catholic moment." Maurin's concerns, in the lines following, were addressed to another generation of Catholic intellectuals, but they strike me as having a perennial quality:

> To blow the dynamite
> of a message
> is the only way
> to make the message dynamic.
> If the Catholic Church
> is not today
> the dominant social force,
> it is because Catholic scholars
> have failed to blow the dynamite
> of the Church.
> Catholic scholars
> have taken the dynamite
> of the Church,
> have wrapped it up
> in nice phraseology,
> placed it in a hermetic container
> and sat on the lid.
> It is about time
> to blow the lid off. . . .

[Cited in Robert Trisco, ed., *Catholics in America 1776–1976* (Washington: National Conference of Catholic Bishops, 1976), p. 216.]

8. For a curmudgeonly argument about the cultural gentility of latter-day American Catholic (indeed, latter-day American religious) intellectuals, cf. John Murray Cuddihy, *No Offense: Civil Religion and Protestant Taste* (New York: Seabury, 1978).

9. Cf. David Tracy, *The Analogical Imagination* (New York: Crossroad, 1981).

10. For an analysis of this point, cf. George Lindbeck, "Scripture, Consensus and Community," in *This World* 23 (Fall 1988), pp. 5–24. This essay develops themes previously adumbrated in Lindbeck's *The Nature of Doctrine* (Philadelphia: Westminster Press, 1984).

11. For the data cited above, cf. Richard John Neuhaus, ed., *Unsecular America* (Grand Rapids: Eerdmans, 1986), pp. 115–58. Even more striking is the analysis of Theodore Caplow and his colleagues in *All Faithful People* (Minneapolis: University of Minnesota Press, 1983), in which the authors, having replicated the "Middletown" studies of the 1930s, conclude that Americans have become *more* religious over the past fifty years. "Middletown" (Muncie, Indiana) is not, of course, all of America. But the Caplow research was sufficiently striking as to move Peter Berger to argue in these blunt terms: "There has been the proposition, which in an earlier part of my own life I supported, that modernization means secularization. I think we can say that the data . . . that Caplow has been producing falsifies that proposition. Period. It has to be thrown out. I have thrown it out. . . . That's how scientific understanding proceeds" (in Neuhaus, ed., *Unsecular America*, pp. 84–85). Figures on religious giving may be found in the *Chronicle of Philanthropy* 1:5 (Dec. 20, 1988), pp. 1, 9; the $41.1 billion cited in this study may be considerably low, given the widely acknowledged tendency of some pastors to under-report donations. Cf. also Andrew M. Greeley, *Religious Indicators 1940–1985* (Cambridge: Harvard University Press, 1989).

12. Wade Clark Roof and William McKinney, *American Mainline Religion: Its Changing Shape and Future* (New Brunswick: Rutgers University Press, 1987), p. 86, emphasis added.

13. Cf. John Shelby Spong, *Living in Sin? A Bishop Rethinks Human Sexuality* (San Francisco: Harper & Row, 1988), pp. 196–207.

14. A now classic headline in the *New York Times* in 1988, noting an annual "Gaia Mass," read, "10 billion algae are borne up the aisle of St. John the Divine to be blessed."

15. On the concept of the "new class" and the arguments surrounding this important (if controversial) analytic construct, cf. R. Bruce-Briggs, ed., *The New Class?* (New Brunswick: Transaction Books, 1979), and Stephen Brint, "Stirrings of an Oppositional Elite? The Social Bases and Historical Trajectory of Upper White Collar Dissent in the United States, 1960–1980," unpublished Ph.D. dissertation, Harvard University, 1982. James Davison Hunter analyzes the new-class/religion nexus at one crucial growing end of American religion in "The New Class and the Young Evangelicals," *The Review of Religious Research* 22:2 (December 1980), pp. 155–69.

16. Cf. the *Proceedings of the Forty-Second Annual Convention of the Catholic Theological Society of America*, in which the report on the workshop "Feminism and Theological Language" includes the following:

Mary Daly figured prominently in this workshop presentation for two reasons. Daly was the first female member of the CTSA to force her entrance into the assembly in 1966, despite threats to call the police. Daly's counterthreat to call the press won the day. Women attending the CTSA today in increasing numbers, presenting papers, and hearing some of our questions being addressed in major sessions, need to remember our brave foresister, Mary Daly, that crone, hag, witch, spinster, fury, amazon who dared to change the character of the CTSA.

While Daly now considers herself a radical post-Christian feminist, she is one of the prime movers of the linguistic turn of feminism and a significant voice from the periphery that cannot be ignored by the revisionist center without peril [*Proceedings*, p. 135].

17. During the civil trial of Father Charles Curran's suit against the Catholic University of America, Father Richard McBrien's testimony was reported as follows:

The Rev. Richard P. McBrien, chairman of the theology department at the University of Notre Dame, testified . . . that only a review by academic peers could determine a theologian's right to teach.

According to prevailing American standards of academic freedom, Father McBrien said, a university could not surrender such judgments to any outside body like the Vatican's Congregation for the Doctrine of the Faith, the body that censured Father Curran.

After Kevin T. Baine, Catholic University's lawyer, quoted statements by Father McBrien defending the right of the church to determine whether some theologians had abandoned authentic Catholic teaching, Father McBrien said that while the church had a right to make such determinations, that did not mean it could enforce them on a university faculty [Peter Steinfels, "Academic Freedom Is Key Issue in Suit," *New York Times*, Dec. 18, 1988, p. 30].

Another aspect of the Curran trial is worth pondering. Father John Courtney Murray, S.J., in whose tradition of American Catholic social thought Father Curran wishes to place himself, spent a considerable part of his academic career trying to disentangle the Church from the notion that state authority ought to be placed at the service of Catholic truth-claims. It is difficult to imagine Father Murray endorsing Father Curran's use of what we used to call the "secular arm" to adjudicate what is, at bottom, an ecclesiological dispute.

18. Cf. my *Tranquillitas Ordinis: The Present Failure and Future Promise of American Catholic Thought on War and Peace* (New York: Oxford University Press, 1987), pp. 177–313. A more recent example of this problem may be found in Professor Gregory Baum's 1986 address to the Catholic Theological Society of America:

With other social critics, I see in the United States three politico-philosophical approaches. The first corresponds to the orientation of the present [i.e., Reagan] administration. It is often euphemistically called neo-conservative. It represents a peculiar union between monetarism and militarism. The neo-conservative political philosophy regards the free market as the essential principle of society, assuring economic growth, personal freedom and the relative justice of equal opportunity. Neo-conservatism wants to remove the influence of the public on economic institutions, shrink the welfare system, weaken labor organizations, reconcile people with existing levels of poverty and unemployment, and foster indifference to the plight of the impoverished nations. Neo-conservatism sees America as the outpost of freedom in the world. And because American society is the highpoint of human cultural evolution, it is argued, the enemies of the free market, the socialists, the people under the power or sway of the Soviet Union, try to humiliate the American people. What is necessary, therefore, is a new love of country, a new nationalism. To defend itself against its enemies, reluctantly, America has taken on the role of a military empire ["The Social Context of American Catholic Theology," in George Kilcourse, ed., *Proceedings of the Forty-First Annual Convention of the Catholic Theological Society of America*, p. 95].

Further evidence of this trend may be found in Professor Jay P. Dolan's review of *Tranquillitas Ordinis* in the *New York Times Book Review* (April 26, 1987), in which Dolan argued, astonishingly, that Catholicism had no "recognizable theory of peace" for "fifteen centuries." This is a judgment whose roots lie, I think, precisely in Dolan's internalization of the Berrigan critique of American Catholicism.

19. The connection between the internalization of the secularization theory and the politicization of the mainline/oldline might be understood in these terms: If we believe that we cannot speak a word of Gospel truth into this radically secularized society, then we are faced with the problem of what to do with the institutions whose primary purpose was traditionally understood to be that proclamation. Well, if we cannot be evangelical, perhaps we can be useful. The terms of "utility" are then adopted from the surrounding culture, which means, since all this was going on in the early 1960s, that the criteria of utility became political, and a very distinctive form of political at that.

20. My friend John Langan, S.J., has warned against a too easy identification of "intellectuals" properly understood with what Langan terms (in a nice mix of whimsy and bite) the *lumpenintelligentsia* as found in, say, Catholic periodical literature. The caution is well taken, but since the cases mentioned just above involve, *inter alia*, such prestigious institutions as the Catholic Theological Society of America, it seems appropriate to describe these problems as something other than problems of vulgarization.

21. The Brogan quote and the Ellis quotes following are from the "Program" of the annual meeting of the Catholic Commission on Intellectual and Cultural Affairs, Maryville College, May 14–15, 1955. Ellis's CCICA paper was subsequently published in full in *Thought* XXX:118 (Autumn 1955), pp. 351–88.

22. Cf. Ellis's introductory note and an excerpt from Bishop Wright's commentary on the Ellis argument in John Tracy Ellis, ed., *Documents of American Catholic History*, vol. 2 (Wilmington: Michael Glazier, 1987), pp. 641–46.

23. For a critique of the empirical basis of Ellis's argument, cf. Andrew M. Greeley, "Nothing But a Loud-Mouthed Irish Priest," in Gregory Baum, ed., *Journeys* (New York: Paulist Press, 1975), pp. 188–90. Greeley had undertaken his doctoral research at the University of Chicago on a theme suggested by William McManus, then superintendent of schools in the Archdiocese of Chicago, who urged Greeley to find out "for the love of God . . . why our kids aren't going to graduate school." What Greeley found, however, was that "Catholics were more likely to go to graduate school than Protestants," a finding that led, Greeley argued, to the collapse of "a lot of conventional wisdom" as well as to the collapse of Greeley's "image with the self-proclaimed liberals of the Church." As Greeley would say of this experience: "I learned a lot [including]: 'Don't believe anything until you've got the data' " (ibid., pp. 189–90).

A generation later, Greeley and his colleagues found even better news to report. By 1973 the survey research indicated,

> There is no such thing as a "Catholic factor" that impedes educational, economic and occupational success. . . . It [i.e., the history of American Catholicism] is a remarkable success story. The American Catholic population has absorbed immigration, war, and depression. It has seized for itself not only parity, but for some groups, in some matters, superiority in American society. The Irish in particular have been, despite their own frequently agonized lamentations,

extraordinarily successful. Unfortunately for American Catholics they have become successful only when success is no longer considered important. When the rest of the society valued educational, occupational, and economic success, Catholics didn't have it. Now that they have achieved it, it seems that the intellectual elites are disposed to write off achievement as the result of selfishness and greed [Andrew M. Greeley, William C. McCready, and Kathleen McCourt, *Catholic Schools in a Declining Church* (Kansas City: Sheed & Ward, 1976), pp. 69, 74].

What Greeley meant by "educational success" here is not, of course, precisely what Ellis meant by "Catholic intellectual life." On the other hand, Greeley's data do suggest that even the now widely deprecated American Catholicism of the 1950s and early 1960s was not predisposing American Catholics to disdain intellectual endeavor.

24. Cf. Murray, *We Hold These Truths*, pp. 52–53.

25. Philip Gleason, "Keeping the Faith in America," in *Keeping the Faith: American Catholicism Past and Present* (Notre Dame: University of Notre Dame Press, 1987), p. 170.

26. Catholic "restorationists" today repeat this error, regarding as "ancient tradition" ideas and practices that are, in truth, about as "ancient" as the restorationists' grandmothers. Conversely, the temptation to ahistoricity in the sense of period-fixation also appears on the contemporary Catholic Left, the difference being that the years 1962–1968 are taken as paradigmatic of The Way Things Ought To Be.

27. Philip Gleason, "Immigrant Assimilation and the Crisis of Americanization," in Gleason, *Keeping the Faith*, pp. 74–76.

28. It should be remembered that Murray's creative extension of natural-law theory on matters of church and state paved the way toward Vatican II's seminal "Declaration on Religious Freedom."

29. In his important study of Murray's thought, J. Leon Hooper argues (in what he understands to be Murray's "later" categories),

If the church is to follow the God who redeems, thereby being true to its own mission *and also true to the core consciousness of human society*, it has to surrender its own group biases (hidden as those might be behind institutional and theological theories and symbols), while at the same time maintaining its own self-consciousness as a people who witness to God's historical presence. Whether or not that is sufficient to hold the solidarity of a siege church, after the siege has ended, remains an open question [J. Leon Hooper, *The Ethics of Discourse* (Washington: Georgetown University Press, 1986), p. 225, emphasis added].

Indeed it does remain an open question, particularly if what I have elsewhere termed the "Murray Project" is taken, as Hooper seems to hint in this passage at least, as a kind of extension of Feuerbach.

30. Rosemary Radford Ruether, "John Paul II and the Growing Alienation of Women from the Church," in Hans Küng and Leonard Swidler, eds., *The Church in Anguish: Has the Vatican Betrayed Vatican II?* (San Francisco: Harper & Row, 1988), pp. 279–83. Given the general thrust of this volume, the question mark in the subtitle seems rather superfluous.

31. Richard P. McBrien, "The Hard-Line Pontiff," *Notre Dame* (Spring 1987), pp. 27–29.

32. McBrien's frequent references to Reginald Garrigou-Lagrange as the direc-

tor of Wojtyla's doctoral dissertation, and thus the putative source of the pope's "ahistorical" world-view, are particularly odd. Shall we conclude from McBrien's own doctoral work on John A. T. Robinson that McBrien is committed to an ecclesiology whose methodological roots and general approach to classic Christian truth-claims may be found in *Honest to God*? McBrien would rightly reject any such suggestion.

The jeremiads launched by Ruether and McBrien remind me of one of the famous nonsense-letters exchanged by Thomas Merton and his friend Robert Lax. Wrote Merton on one occasion,

> I am living in and with a hot water bottle on the elbows. I am truly spry and full of fun, but am pursued by the vilifications of progressed Catholics. Mark my word man there is no uglier species on the face of the earth than progressed Catholics, mean, frivol, ungainly, inarticulate, venomous, and bursting at the seams with progress into the secular cities and the Teilhardian subways. The Ottavianis was bad but these are infinitely worse. You wait and see [Thomas Merton and Robert Lax, *A Catch of Anti-Letters*, ed. Patrick Hart (Kansas City: Sheed, Andrews and McMeel, 1978), p. 110; Merton's letter was dated January 26, 1967, a little less than two years before his death].

33. Cf. Alasdair MacIntyre, *After Virtue* (Notre Dame: University of Notre Dame Press, 1981).

34. Cf. *Habits of the Heart: Individualism and Commitment in American Life* (Berkeley: University of California Press, 1984).

35. Cf. Jeffrey Stout, *Ethics After Babel: The Languages of Morals and Their Discontents* (Boston: Beacon Press, 1988).

36. Cf. Alasdair MacIntyre, *Whose Justice? Which Rationality?* (Notre Dame: University of Notre Dame Press, 1988). It is (at least) ironic that MacIntyre, arguably the most influential voice in the past decade's debate over the reconstitution of moral philosophy, has "rediscovered" Thomas Aquinas at precisely the moment when the mainstream of American Catholic moral theology continues its flight from a natural-law-informed ethic.

37. Cf. Michael Novak, *The Spirit of Democratic Capitalism* (New York: Simon & Schuster, 1982); Michael Novak, *Freedom with Justice* (San Francisco: Harper & Row, 1984).

38. Cf. Michael Sandel, *Liberalism and the Limits of Justice* (Cambridge: Cambridge University Press, 1982).

39. In, for example, Kirk's *The Roots of American Order*, first paperback edition (Malibu: Pepperdine University Press, 1978).

40. William Lee Miller, *The First Liberty: Religion and the American Republic* (New York: Knopf, 1986), pp. 145–46.

41. Aidan Nichols, O.P., *The Theology of Joseph Ratzinger* (Edinburgh: T & T Clark, 1988), pp. 294–96.

42. Cf. Neuhaus, *The Catholic Moment*, especially pp. 126 ff.

43. Ibid., p. 126.

44. Lindbeck's work is cited in note 10 of this chapter. Cf. also Thomas C. Oden, "Toward a Theologically Informed Renewal of American Protestantism: Propositions for Debate Attested by Classical Arguments," in Richard John Neuhaus, ed., *The Believable Futures of American Protestantism* (Grand Rapids: Eerdmans, 1988), pp. 72–102.

45. A move in this direction will require, as one modest but important

component, an end to the pope-baiting noted above. I remember being told by an eminent Lutheran systematic theologian that attending the 1987 CTSA convention at the Sheraton Society Hill Hotel in Philadelphia put him in mind of a Southern Baptist convention in the bad old days—every time the pope's name was mentioned, a wave of titters and hisses resonated through the assembled crowd. The Lutheran in question was not being ironic, about either the atmosphere or the locale. Getting beyond pope-baiting won't solve much of anything, but it might help create a psychological atmosphere in which the urgent question of the nature of the authoritative can be more seriously engaged.

46. See my *Catholicism and the Renewal of American Democracy*, pp. 205 ff., for a fuller discussion.

47. Examples of how this might be done on a number of fevered issues may be found in my *Catholicism and the Renewal of American Democracy*.

48. For one cut at exploring this new definition of "public Church," cf. Archbishop J. Francis Stafford's pastoral letter "This Home of Freedom," *This World* 18 (Summer 1987), pp. 84–105.

49. H. Richard Niebuhr, *Christ and Culture* (New York: Harper & Row, 1951).

50. Brigitte Berger and Peter L. Berger, "Our Conservatism and Theirs," *Commentary* 82:4 (October 1986), pp. 63–64.

51. John B. Breslin, S.J., "Introduction," in Breslin, ed., *The Substance of Things Hoped For* (New York: Doubleday Image Books, 1988), pp.xii-xiii.

52. Ibid.

53. David Tracy, "On Hope as a Theological Virtue in American Catholic Theology," in Küng and Swidler, *The Church in Anguish*, p. 272.

54. Karl Rahner, "The Church's Angry Old Men [Interview for Radio Saarland, Munich, April 3, 1982]" in *Karl Rahner in Dialogue: Conversations and Interviews*, ed. Paul Imhof and Herbert Biallowons, trans. ed. Harvey Egan (New York: Crossroad, 1986), pp. 332–33.

55. She did read Rahner, though, and, expressing an opinion common to tens of thousands before and after her, commented: "[Rahner] is great but difficult to read. I read every sentence about three times and then have trouble connecting it with the next one. But every now and then I get the impact . . ." (Letter to Janet McKane, in *The Habit of Being*, pp. 520–21). Appropriately enough, the work to which she was referring here was Rahner's *On the Theology of Death*.

CHAPTER SIX
Capturing the Story Line

1. Cf. "Cushing Papers Found," *American Catholic Studies Newsletter* 17:1 (Spring 1990), p. 2.

2. The same charge was, of course, vigorously pressed in secular garb in the 1950s by such polemicists as Paul Blanshard.

3. Cited in John Tracy Ellis, *American Catholicism*, 2nd ed., rev. (Chicago: University of Chicago Press, 1969), p. 151.

4. Cf. Richard John Neuhaus, "Those Turbulent Bishops," in *National Review*, December 31, 1989, pp. 32–33.

5. Cited in Robert Brugger, *Maryland: A Middle Temperament* (Baltimore:

Johns Hopkins University Press, 1988), pp. 20–21. Cf. also Donald Marquand Dozer, *Portrait of the Free State: A History of Maryland* (Cambridge: Tidewater Publishers, 1976), pp. 90–92. The Maryland Act was, by our standards, quite inadequate, as it was an act for religious toleration among Christians only. But as Brugger writes, for all its weaknesses, "the measure marked a notable departure from Old World oppression."

6. The vitality of the "Carroll Church" as the paradigm of American Catholicism was evident as recently as 1961, when Lawrence J. Shehan had the following to say during his installation as coadjutor archbishop of Baltimore and John Carroll's eleventh successor:

> In coming back to Baltimore [Shehan, a Baltimore native, had been bishop of Bridgeport, Connecticut, from 1953 to 1961], I am deeply conscious of returning to the main source of the great traditions of the American Church. Those traditions center in the person of John Carroll, our first bishop and archbishop. Not only did Carroll firmly establish the ecclesiastical structure which has served so well the Church in this country; he also more than any other person gave origin to those noble traditions which have given to the American Church its special character. . . .
>
> The tradition which comes most vividly to mind at the present time when Catholics are figuring so prominently in national life and in public controversies is the church-state relationship which sprang chiefly from John Carroll and has become for us a sort of sacred heritage. Shortly after George Washington had been elected our first President, Carroll, himself recently consecrated bishop, joined four of the most prominent lay Catholics of this country . . . in addressing to the President a letter of congratulations on his unanimous election to the highest honor within the giving of his fellow citizens. They expressed not only their satisfaction at the state of affairs which had come into existence under his leadership but also their confidence that as long as this country continued to preserve her independence they and their fellow Catholics would have every title to claim from her justice, the equal right of citizenship as the price of their blood and of their common exertion for the country's defense. To this letter Washington replied that he hoped that America would ever appear foremost among the nations of the world in examples of justice and liberality and that Americans would never forget the important part Catholics had taken in the accomplishment of their revolution and in the establishment of their government. Thus it was that Carroll helped to establish that spirit of devoted loyalty on the part of American Catholics and that spirit of justice, confidence, and friendliness on the part of the Federal Government which has characterized the history of the Church in the United States [Lawrence Cardinal Shehan, *A Blessing of Years* (Notre Dame: University of Notre Dame Press, 1982), p. 129].

Shehan, as archbishop, would be quick to act on another legacy of the "Carroll Church" by inaugurating the Catholic world's first diocesan ecumenical commission in the spring of 1962.

7. Cf. Gerald P. Fogarty, S.J., *The Vatican and the American Hierarchy from 1870 to 1965* (Wilmington: Michael Glazier, 1985), p. 1.

8. Cf. Marvin R. O'Connell, *John Ireland and the American Catholic Church* (St. Paul: Minnesota Historical Society Press, 1988, pp. 269–71).

9. For a critically sympathetic portrait of this not altogether sympathetic figure, cf. John Tracy Ellis, *Catholic Bishops: A Memoir* (Wilmington: Michael Glazier, 1983), pp. 67–77. On hearing of O'Connell's nomination to the College

of Cardinals in 1911, Gibbons is said to have wept in frustration and chagrin (Fogarty, *The Vatican and the American Hierarchy*, p. 205).

10. Cf. James Hennesey, S.J., *The First Council of the Vatican: The American Experience* (New York: Herder and Herder, 1963) and *American Catholics* (New York: Oxford University Press, 1981).

11. Cf. Gerald P. Fogarty, S.J., *The Vatican and the Americanist Crisis: Denis J. O'Connell, American Agent in Rome, 1885–1903* (Rome: Universita Gregoriana Editrice, 1974), and *The Vatican and the American Hierarchy*.

12. Cf. O'Connell, *John Ireland and the American Catholic Church*.

13. Indeed, in this later work Fogarty drew on the research he had previously done for his volume on Gibbons's Roman agent, Denis J. O'Connell.

14. San Francisco: Harper & Row, 1989.

15. New York: Doubleday, 1983.

16. That the "new history" has its limits is made clear by a story told by the eminent historian Gertrude Himmelfarb:

> A few years ago, in a discussion of recent trends in the writing of history, one young historian proudly described his work as being on the "cutting edge of the discipline." He was writing a study of a New England town toward the end of the eighteenth century, an "in-depth" analysis of the life of its inhabitants: their occupations and earnings, living and working conditions, familial and sexual relations, habits, attitudes, and social institutions. He regretted that he had to confine himself to that one town, but some of his colleagues were doing comparable studies of other towns and their collective efforts would constitute a "total history" of that time and place.
>
> I asked him whether his study, or their collective studies, had any bearing on what I, admittedly not a specialist in American history, took to be the most momentous event of that time and place, indeed one of the most momentous events in all of modern history: the founding of the United States of America, the first major republic of modern times. He conceded that from his themes and sources—parish registers, tax rolls, census reports, legal records, polling lists, land titles—he could not "get to," as he said, the founding of the United States. But he denied that this was the crucial event I took it to be. What was crucial were the lives and experiences of the mass of the people. . . . My rebuttal—that even ordinary people (perhaps most of all ordinary people) had been profoundly affected in the most ordinary aspects of their lives by the founding of the republic, by political events, institutions, and ideas that had created a new polity and with it a new society—seemed to him naïve and old-fashioned [*The New History and the Old* (Cambridge: Belknap Press, 1987), pp. 13–14].

We may expect similar historiographic attitudes to shape the retelling of the story of American Catholicism in the future, particularly under the impact of "feminist studies."

17. On "discontinuity" as a contemporary Catholic hermeneutical device, cf. Philip Gleason, "History, Historical Consciousness, and Present-Mindedness," in *Keeping the Faith: American Catholicism Past and Present* (Notre Dame: University of Notre Dame Press, 1987), p. 206.

18. Christopher J. Kauffman, gen. ed. (New York: Macmillan, 1989).

19. James Hennesey, S.J., "An Eighteenth Century Bishop: John Carroll of Baltimore," in Gerald P. Fogarty, S.J., ed., *Patterns of Episcopal Leadership* (New York: Macmillan, 1989), p. 34.

20. Writes Dolan:

With the spirit of independence, so manifest in the 1780s, gone, Carroll became increasingly dependent on the Papacy. All throughout his career as a leader in the American Catholic community, he sought to maintain a balance between being a loyal American and a faithful Roman Catholic. It was a delicate balancing act; in his younger years, as a priest, he leaned toward the American spirit of independence; in his later years, as bishop, he moved closer to the stance of a Roman Catholic for whom the Papacy was the vital center of the Church. Though he still held firm to his belief that the authority of the Papacy was limited to "things purely spiritual," he no longer supported the idea of an *independent American Catholic Church* [Dolan, *The American Catholic Experience*, p. 113, emphasis added].

No one familiar with the story of John Carroll's episcopate will deny that the founding father had frequent moments of exasperation with the authorities in Rome. But Dolan's image of the "balancing act" between "being a loyal American and a faithful Roman Catholic" ill fits Carroll's circumstances, and in fact says rather less about Carroll than about Dolan's sense of the American Catholic present. Here, one suspects, the tension perceived by Professor Dolan is between being an American loyal to the canons of liberalism as defined by the American academic elite and being a faithful Roman Catholic. But why the preoccupations of some in the contemporary American Catholic intellectual guild should be retrospectively projected onto John Carroll (who had problems enough of his own!) is not entirely clear.

21. Margaret Mary Reher, *Catholic Intellectual Life in America* (New York: Macmillan, 1989), pp. 9, 7.

22. Thomas W. Spalding, *The Premier See: A History of the Archdiocese of Baltimore, 1789–1989* (Baltimore: Johns Hopkins University Press, 1989), p. 321. Spalding's second citation, about "providential hosts," is taken from William M. Halsey's *The Survival of American Innocence: Catholicism in an Era of Disillusionment, 1920–1940* (Notre Dame: University of Notre Dame Press, 1980). The Halsey volume, like Dolan's *American Catholic Experience*, is a major historiographic text for Catholic revisionism.

Garry Wills, whose childhood in the "Catholic ghetto" does not seem to have seriously impeded his academic or journalistic success, sang a rather different tune fifteen or so years ago. Then, in a finely chiseled essay, "Memories of a Catholic Boyhood," he wrote, "It was a ghetto, undeniably. But not a bad ghetto to grow up in" (*Bare Ruined Choirs* [New York: Doubleday, 1972], p. 37).

23. Cf. John Tracy Ellis, "American Catholics and the Intellectual Life," *Thought* XXX:118 (Autumn 1955), pp. 351–88.

24. Happily, others are paying attention, including Joseph P. Chinnici, in his *Living Stones: The History and Structure of Catholic Spiritual Life in the United States* (New York: Macmillan, 1989), a volume in the Bicentennial History series.

Cf. also the interesting, occasionally quirky, and at some points (as on American Catholic anti-communism) just plain wrongheaded study of "Catholic romanticism" during this period, James Terence Fisher's *The Catholic Counterculture in America, 1933–1962* (Chapel Hill: University of North Carolina Press, 1989).

25. Cf. Dolan, *The American Catholic Experience*, pp. 451–54; Wills, "Church Against World," in *Bare Ruined Choirs*, pp. 266–72.

26. Cf. Shehan, *A Blessing of Years*, pp. 239–40.

27. On Curley, cf. Spalding, *The Premier See*, pp. 321–85. On Mundelein, cf.

Edward R. Kantowicz, *Corporation Sole: Cardinal Mundelein and Chicago Catholicism* (Notre Dame: University of Notre Dame Press, 1983).

28. Spalding, *The Premier See*, pp. 322, 384.

29. Spalding is similarly cautious about buying the revisionist view of John Carroll whole cloth, referring in *The Premier See*, and in direct citation of Dolan, to "the 'republican blueprint' [Carroll] *is said to have drawn*" (*The Premier See*, pp. 19–20, emphasis added). On the other hand, Spalding is thoroughly revisionist on the question of lay trusteeism, rereading the controversies of the early nineteenth century on the ownership of church property through the filters of post–Vatican II sensibilities and concerns for lay participation in church affairs.

30. Frederick Crews, "The Parting of the Twains," *New York Review of Books*, July 20, 1989, p. 39. Philip Gleason styles this phenomenon "emphatic present-mindedness" or "uncritical present-mindedness," which is "almost certain to produce distortions in historical work. The reason is that it assumes that the past can be *forced* to speak to us on our terms, that all we need to do is formulate 'relevant' questions and address them to the past in a sufficiently peremptory manner."

"But that," Professor Gleason goes on to warn, "is no way to get a bygone age to yield its secrets. If we insist on blustering into the past, waving our search warrants of relevance and announcing that we intend to 'ransack' it for our present needs, we will encounter nothing there but our own reverberating obsessions" ("History, Historical Consciousness, and Present-Mindedness," pp. 214–15).

31. Philip Gleason, "The New Americanism in Catholic Historiography," unpublished paper presented at a meeting of the Organization of American Historians, Washington, D.C., March 24, 1990 (emphasis added).

32. Cf. Margaret Mary Reher, "The Church and the Kingdom of God in America: The Ecclesiology of the Americanists," unpublished Ph.D. dissertation, Fordham University, 1972.

33. San Francisco: Harper & Row, 1989.

34. In *Our Unfinished Business: The U.S. Catholic Bishops' Letters on Peace and the Economy* (New York: Pantheon, 1990), Phillip Berryman makes this point from the perspective of the Catholic left: the NCCB/USCC "consensus" model of decision-making impedes the rapid development of a truly radical Catholic social witness. Berryman, however, seems willing to work on these matters incrementally, perhaps because he understands the utility of a liberal stalking horse (even one built by "consensus") for his own more radical agenda.

Although Berryman expends six pages of his slim volume in a rather silly analysis of my *Tranquillitas Ordinis: The Present Failure and Future Promise of American Catholic Thought on War and Peace* (New York: Oxford, 1987), I think he is on to something in his critique of the bishops' style of decision-making, in which the unity of the bishops' conference, rather than the truth of the matters under debate, is the decisive issue. Berryman and I would differ on where that truth resides on matters such as U.S. foreign policy, environmentalism, and the feminist agenda. But we might share the conviction that splitting the difference, so to speak, is not the way for *religious* leaders to decide issues at the crossroads of religious conviction, moral reasoning, and public policy.

35. Donald Pellotte's *John Courtney Murray: Theologian in Conflict* (New York: Paulist Press, 1975) is an interesting and useful study of Murray's work on church-state issues and the question of religious liberty, but does not engage Murray's

many other interests, or the range of his engagements with political and intellectual agencies and organizations.

36. Thus the interpretation of Murray adduced by J. Leon Hooper in *The Ethics of Discourse* (Washington: Georgetown University Press, 1986).

37. The Catholic right would, of course, insist that this business of "majestic changelessness" had nothing mythic about it at all. Nonetheless, we see here, again, a curious confluence between the new historiography and the contemporary Catholic right, who share (even as they differ in interpreting) a basic image for the pre-Conciliar Church.

38. The truth of the matter is that women were immensely powerful in pre-Conciliar American Catholicism, if power is measured by direct and continuing effect on people's daily lives. The mandate of the Third Plenary Council of Baltimore (1884) that every parish must have a Catholic school, the pattern established in large urban dioceses of building the new school (and convent) before the new church (and rectory), and the flowering of vocations to the religious life among American Catholic women worked together to produce an institution that, by the second or third decade of the twentieth century, offered women far more scope for the exercise of real power than any other in the United States.

Index of Names